really easy defence

This book is for players who have been playing bridge for a year or two. It's for those players who have just realised that the cards partner is playing can carry a message. Noticing the cards and giving them a meaning is when a player becomes a real defender.

Most players just put a card on the table, their lowest one if partner is winning the trick, their highest one if they are called upon to win the trick. Why should it matter which card is used?

Read this book and your eyes will be opened. Read it with your partner and you will become the sharpest defenders in town. Opponents will start to worry when they play against you, the pair who get every contract at least one down – actually that is impossible to achieve but it should be your aim.

Really Easy Defence contains a selection of the good simple ideas that have been developed by successful players over the years, chosen from a plethora of possibilities. Trust your teachers and their choices, and you will have a comprehensive set of defensive tools.

John Pain
EBU Teachers' Association Manager

Sandra Landy
Series Editor

Other books in the Really Easy Bridge Series.

Really Easy Bidding 2nd ed   1999 reprinted 2001
Really Easy Play in No Trumps 1999
Really Easy Practice 1   1999
Really Easy Mistakes   2000
Really Easy Practice 2   2000
Really Easy Modern Acol   2001
Really Easy Play with Trumps   2001

© English Bridge Union Ltd 2002

ISBN 0 9506279 9 2

Designed by Milestone Strategic Creative Design of Beaconsfield
Typeset by Wakewing of High Wycombe
Printed and bound by Buckingham Colour Group Limited

The English Bridge Union
Broadfields
Bicester Road
Aylesbury HP19 8AZ
Tel: 01296 317217
Fax: 01296 317220
Email: bfa@ebu.co.uk

Really Easy Defence

English Bridge Union

contents

1 thinking about defence

In a typical session of bridge, you will be declarer on one hand in four. On another you will be dummy, your turn to get the drinks! But half the time you and partner will be defending, trying to beat the bid contract.

Look carefully at a pack of cards. You will see that some of the court cards are carrying weapons; they are the leaders of the army that will take on the battle for the contract. In bridge, you and your partner – in this book you are called WE – West and East – take on the opposition, who are called North and South. What you have to do is very clear:

Aim to beat every opposition contract by at least one trick.

Some contracts can't be beaten however hard you try. But many can and if you start down the warpath believing that you can beat the contract, you are much more likely to succeed in your mission.

Why is defence difficult?

When you are declarer, you can see your side's combined assets very clearly. Dummy is on the table and you can play those 26 cards to your side's best advantage.

As a defender you cannot see your partner's hand, but you have to co-operate to defeat the contract. You cannot kick him under the table to pass a message. You can only send messages by the cards you play. Each card you play carries clues about your hand. Partner can see his own hand and dummy so this helps him work out what declarer holds.

You have to watch partner's cards, which are signals to you, to read the messages being sent. You must decide what to do with the information partner tries to give you.

Of course, to make useful signals, you and your partner must agree what those signals will be or you won't understand each other.

Sometimes defence is easy. As West, you hold:

♠ A K Q J 10   South opens 1NT.
♥ 4 3 2   You pass and North raises to 3NT.
♦ 4 3 2   What should you lead?
♣ 3 2

With five top spades, you can lead them out to take the first five tricks. Remember, your mission is to get declarer one down.

This hand is harder because you cannot beat the contract on your own.

♠ 10 9 6 5   As West you hold this hand. North
♥ K 9 7 5   opens 1♦. South responds 1NT, North
♦ 4 3   raises to 3NT.
♣ 8 6 4   What should you lead?

Choosing the lead is difficult because you have no clues about the cards your partner holds. North has diamonds, so it is probably wrong to lead them, but what about the other three suits?

A spade or a heart look better leads as you have more cards in those suits – but which one is a guess. The card you lead from your chosen suit is a message that helps partner work out what you hold and hence what declarer has.

If only you could see your partner's hand it would be so easy. Just look what partner holds opposite the problem hand. Now it is very plain that spades are our side's best suit.

♠ K Q J 8 7   A spade lead is very likely to beat 3NT.
♥ 3 2   Isn't there a way for partner to tell you
♦ 8 7 6 5   what to do?
♣ K 3

In this case there is. Your partner could have overcalled one diamond with one spade. The hand has just nine points but it has a good spade suit with three honours – the sort of suit you want partner to lead. An honour is an ace, king, queen, jack or 10.

Overcall on a good suit to get the defence off to a flying start.

This book is about defenders' play, not bidding. Read *Really Easy Bidding* or *Really Easy Modern Acol* to learn more about overcalling.

About this book

In this book our aim is to beat every declarer's contract by one trick. Don't worry about getting any contract more than one down. Chapters 2–9 are mainly about defending no trump contracts, suit contracts being covered in later chapters.

- ■ South is always declarer.

- ■ North is always dummy.

- ■ West and East are the defensive team, called WE in this book. WE are the team who, working together, will beat declarer's contracts.

- ■ West always makes the opening lead, as South is always declarer.

- ■ East is always in third seat, playing after dummy.

Don't be confused by the fact that in this book you will sometimes be West and sometimes East. It cannot be avoided. You have to learn how to send and receive signals from both sides of the table. Before you tackle a problem, make sure you know where you are sitting today!

Throughout the book, x is used to denote a small, less significant card. So if you see ♥K Q J x, the x might be any small card.

Practise as you go

This book contains activities to help you learn.

Practise is to help you remember the ideas and rules explained in the Chapter. Not only do they reinforce the words, some people find it easier to learn by example.

A Quiz has problems based on the current topic. Cover up the suggested answer before tackling the problems.

At the end of the book you will find Case Studies – linked problems that draw together a number of themes from different chapters.

Try them all!

2 choosing the card to lead

The defence has one big advantage – they fire the first shot in the battle by making the opening lead. Sadly, there is no sure way to choose the right lead every time, but let's start by looking at some of the basic principles.

In no trumps lead a long suit to set up winners.

You lead your longest suit because you can set up more winners in that suit. WE may take the first five tricks straight off, but more often declarer has stoppers that must be driven out to set up our winners. In that case you will need an entry to get in to cash those winners. The next chapter looks at how to choose the suit to lead. This chapter is about which card you and your partner agree to lead in the chosen suit.

Leading from a sequence of honours

A solid sequence of honours, that is three, four or five touching cards, provides a good lead. WE lead the top card to show the strength of the sequence. From K Q J 10, lead the king, telling partner this is your highest card in the suit. If neither your partner nor dummy has the ace, partner will know that declarer must have it.

The card that is underlined is the one you should lead. To choose any other card will only mislead partner. The lead of an honour card shows the honour below as well.

Examples where the top card is led:

A̲ K Q   A̲ K Q J 10   K̲ Q J   Q̲ J 10   J̲ 10 9 8   1̲0̲ 9 8 x

A broken sequence is two touching honours then one missing then the next card. The top card of a broken sequence is nearly as good a lead.

Examples where the top card is led:

A̲ K J   A̲ K J 9   K̲ Q 10 9   Q̲ J 9 x   J̲ 10 8 7   1̲0̲ 9 7 6

Holding an interior sequence, that is an honour followed by a gap, followed by a sequence, lead the top of the interior sequence. This is a good but not so safe lead against a no trump contract. It would not necessarily be a good lead against a suit contract.

Examples where the top of interior sequence is led:

A J 10 9   A Q J 10   K J 10 9   K 10 9 8   Q 10 9 8

Against a suit contract it would be wrong to lead the queen from A Q J 10 or jack from A J 10 9, since WE never underlead an ace against a suit contract (see page 71). Other honour leads are the same against a suit.

An exception to that rule is that occasionally, usually when leading partner's suit, you might lead from a doubleton honour holding. Lead the honour, e.g. king from Kx, queen from Qx etc.

Lead fourth highest from a long suit

When you don't have a suit with a good honour sequence, you normally lead your longest suit. Lead a low card hoping that partner can help with a useful honour or two. By agreement you should lead the fourth highest – that is the fourth one down starting from the top. Examples where the fourth best is led:

Q 10 8 6 4 2   K J 8 4 2   Q 9 7 2   A 8 7 6

Holding a suit headed by a two-honour sequence, such as A K or K Q or Q J, you treat this as a long suit in no trumps and lead the fourth highest. In Chapter 4, you will find out how to understand a fourth highest lead. But remember leads are different against a suit contract (see Chapter 10).

Sometimes you lead from a 3-card suit, perhaps because partner has bid it or because every other lead seems worse. If you do, lead your lowest card if you have an honour, e.g. 5 from K 6 5.

Leading a king against no trumps

Sometimes one partner wants to send the other a very special message. 'I have an excellent suit, do you hold any useful cards in this suit?'

Suppose you have ♥A K J 10 9 3. What should you lead? Maybe you should play ♥A and ♥K hoping the queen will drop? Maybe the lead of ♥J is best, letting declarer's queen win but hoping partner has a heart to lead back later to cash the winners. Maybe it is best to lead ♥A then switch, hoping partner gets in and returns the suit. But partner might have had the queen all the time. The solution is surprising.

The special lead of a king in no trumps asks partner to play any honour that is held, be it the ace, queen, jack or ten.

Without an honour, it asks partner to give a count signal, by playing a higher card then a lower one with an even number of cards. A low card then a higher card shows an odd number of cards. There will be more on count signals later in the book (see Chapter 7).

Here are some examples where West leads the king. Nearly always West has four honours, so to unblock shows where the fifth honour card is. Check how it works with these examples.

West holds	East has	Play	Why
♥A K̲ J 10 8	♥Q 9 4	♥Q	Play your honour, as requested.
♥K̲ Q 10 9 7	♥J 4 2	♥J	Play your honour, as requested.
♥A K̲ Q 10	♥J 4 2	♥J	Play your honour, as requested.
♥K̲ Q J 10 9	♥A 3	♥A	Play your honour, as requested.
♥A K̲ J 10 8	♥7 2	♥7	Play a high card to show two.
♥A K̲ J 10 8	♥7 6 2	♥2	Play a low card to show three.
♥A K̲ J 10 8	♥7 6 4 2	♥6	Play a high card to show four.

Let's look at an example of how leading a king works:

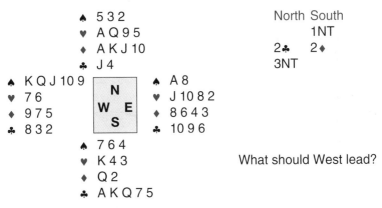

♠ 5 3 2
♥ A Q 9 5
♦ A K J 10
♣ J 4

♠ K Q J 10 9
♥ 7 6
♦ 9 7 5
♣ 8 3 2

N
W E
S

♠ A 8
♥ J 10 8 2
♦ 8 6 4 3
♣ 10 9 6

♠ 7 6 4
♥ K 4 3
♦ Q 2
♣ A K Q 7 5

North	South
	1NT
2♣	2♦
3NT	

What should West lead?

Against 3NT, West should lead a spade. Spades is the only suit where West can set up winners. In theory it doesn't matter which spade West leads as they are all equal. But every card led sends a message to East.

The ♠Q lead says 'I have a sequence of spades headed by ♠Q, either ♠Q J 10 9 or ♠Q J 9 8, or occasionally ♠A Q J 10. I definitely have ♠J.'

The ♠J lead says 'I have a sequence of spades headed by ♠J. It might be ♠J 10 9 8 or ♠J 10 9 x or I could have ♠A J 10 9 or ♠K J 10 9.'

To lead ♠10 says much the same. Either it is top of a sequence, showing ♠9 and denying ♠J, or it is part of an internal sequence, such as ♠A 10 9 8, ♠K 10 9 8 or ♠Q 10 9 8.

To lead ♠9 shows a doubleton, a suit with NO honours at all!

To lead ♠K says 'I have a really good suit, missing an honour. If you hold that honour, please play it.' Look at the deal above. If West leads ♠K and East plays ♠8 on the first trick, West will play another spade, East has to win ♠A, but now has no small spade left to play to West, to make the remaining spades. East is said to have blocked the suit.

But if East plays ♠A at trick one, as requested, he has ♠8 to lead back to partner. Five spade tricks means 3NT is one down.

Leading an ace against no trumps

Since the king is led from strong holdings like A K J 10 9 against no trump contracts, when is the ace led?

It is very rare to lead an unsupported ace. Aces are good for killing other honours or for providing an entry to established winners. An unsupported ace is normally only led when partner has bid the suit. An ace lead nearly always shows the king but the suit is not so strong.

The ace might be led from A K x, A K J x, A K Q x or A K x x – suits where you don't want partner to unblock an honour, but want to know if partner likes the suit. You want partner to encourage or discourage.

What card should you play when your partner leads an ace? We will look at signalling in more detail very shortly, but for now remember, you play a high card if you like the lead and a low one if you don't.

Look at these examples, the lead is ♣A and dummy has ♣4 3 2

You hold	You play
♣Q J 10 9	♣Q. Partner has found a great lead. The ♣Q shows ♣J as well and says 'Please continue'.
♣Q 9 7 6 5	♣9. You can't spare ♣Q this time but play the biggest card you can.
♣J 9 7 6 5	♣9 to encourage. If partner has ♣A K x and dummy ♣4 3 2, declarer can only have ♣Q x.
♣Q 7 5	♣7 to encourage and hope partner has 4+ cards in the suit.
♣6 5	♣5, the smallest card, to discourage partner.
♣10 7 6 5	♣7. This is hard. Unless you want partner to play another suit you should encourage.

If you like partner's lead but you are not winning the trick, play a high card to be encouraging.

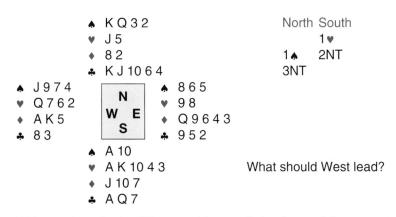

```
        ♠ K Q 3 2              North  South
        ♥ J 5                         1♥
        ♦ 8 2                  1♠      2NT
        ♣ K J 10 6 4          3NT
♠ J 9 7 4          ♠ 8 6 5
♥ Q 7 6 2    N     ♥ 9 8
♦ A K 5    W   E   ♦ Q 9 6 4 3
♣ 8 3        S     ♣ 9 5 2
        ♠ A 10
        ♥ A K 10 4 3          What should West lead?
        ♦ J 10 7
        ♣ A Q 7
```

With two 4-card suits, West would normally lead one of them
against 3NT. But here South has bid hearts, showing at least four
and North has bid spades, also showing at least four cards. We
try to avoid suits bid by the opponents because the chance of
setting winners up in them is far lower. Look what happens on this
deal, if either a heart or spade is led. Either gives away a trick.

West might consider leading a diamond or a club. Either could be
right; it depends what partner holds. But West has ten points and
opponents will have 25 or more between them, so East has at
most five points.

West's few points won't be enough to make lots of club winners,
but in conjunction with West's ♦A K they might just make five
diamond tricks. West should lead ♦A to look around and to ask
partner what he thinks about diamonds.

East can show he likes diamonds by playing a suitably large card,
♦9 is best on the actual deal. Now West will continue with ♦K and
then ♦5. The defence can cash five tricks before declarer gets
the lead.

It is important to lead ♦A. It would be a disaster if West led ♦K
and East, as instructed, played ♦Q!

Leading from suits without any honours

With a singleton (one card) you have no choice.

With a doubleton (two cards) lead the higher, e.g. 7 from 7 5. Of course you have to play the five on the next round of the suit.

With a trebleton (three cards) lead the middle card, e.g. 6 from 9 6 5 and play the 9 on the next round. This is often called MUD standing for Middle Up Down, the order the cards are played.

With four or more worthless cards lead the second highest, e.g. the 7 from 9 7 5 3 and play the 3, the original fourth highest when the suit is next played. This shows a 4-card holding where MUD shows a 3-card holding.

Summary

- Against no trump contracts, lead your longest suit to set up winners.

- WE agree on which card to lead from a given holding. This can help partner work out what the opening leader might hold.

- WE lead the top card from a solid sequence of honours.

- WE lead the top card of the sequence from an interior sequence.

- Otherwise WE lead the fourth highest card from a suit headed by one or more honours.

- WE lead the top card from a doubleton.

- WE lead the second card down from other suits without honours. Playing the highest card on the next round shows a 3-card suit.

- The lead of a king sends a special message. Please unblock any honour you hold. If you haven't got an honour, please give me a count signal.

- Usually leads of 9s or 8s show a worthless suit.

- A low card shows a suit with honours (unless it is from shortage).

Leading against a no trump contract is not the same as leading against a suit contract. The differences are explained in Chapter 10.

Practise your leading

Cover up the last column. Assuming you decide to lead this suit against a no trump contract, which card would be the normal lead? Would it be the same lead against a suit contract?

Holding in suit	Card led against NT	System lead
8 5		8
8 6 2		6 then 8, a MUD lead
10 9 8 7		10 as the 10 is an honour
8 7 6 5		7 then 5
8 6 4 3 2		6 then the 3 then the 2
K 7 5 3		3
Q 10 9 7 2		10, top, interior sequence
K J 10 9 8 2		J, top, interior sequence
A K 7 6 4		6 v NT, A v suit
K Q J 8 7		K
K Q		K
K J 3		3
K Q 3 2		2 v NT, K v suit
A Q 10 9 8		10 v NT, A v suit
J 10 9 8		J
K Q 10 9 8		K, top of broken sequence
A J 10 8 5		J v NT, A v suit
A K Q 3		A
K 10 9 8 5		10
Q J 9 8 6		Q
J 9 8 5		5
A 6 4 3		3 v NT, A v suit

3 choosing the suit to lead

It's all very well knowing which card to lead from a particular holding, but it does not tell you which of the four suits to choose. Before making a lead, always stop and think about the clues that are available to you.

Leading when there are clues to help

Clue One – Look at the cards you hold

The best clue when choosing the lead is the hand you hold. With nothing else to guide you, lead the suit where you can set up tricks. If you lead from ♥K Q alone, you will set up only one trick. If you lead from ♥K Q J 10 9, you can cash five tricks if partner has the ♥A or you will set up four tricks when you have driven out declarer's ♥A.

Clue Two – Opponents must have bid something

The opponents' bidding is often helpful. It can tell you:

- How many points the opponents hold. If 1NT is opened and everybody passes, dummy will have no more than ten points. So if you have seven points, you know partner has at least nine.

- The suits to avoid leading. If a suit is bid and rebid, or it is bid and supported, it is rarely right to lead this suit. This lead is much more likely to help declarer rather than the defence.

- What opponents don't have. If North raises 1NT straight to 3NT without using Stayman, he rarely has a 4-card major. Neither North nor South will have a 5-card major.

- What opponents don't bid. If South replies 1NT to an opening 1♦, it is unlikely South has a 4-card major.

Clue Three – Partner has bid

If partner overcalls, lead partner's suit. When no trumps have been bid after the overcall, opponents probably have stoppers. Lead the suit to drive out the stoppers and set up winners for partner.

Partner overcalls

Remember, you are West on all these hands.

♠ 9 6	West	North	East	South
♥ Q J 10 9 8	pass	1♣	1♠	3NT
♦ 4 3 2				
♣ 10 6 4	Lead ♠9 – partner's suit.			

Sometimes you have a good suit of your own. You should only lead it if you have an entry, which you will need to get in to cash your winners.

♠ A 6	West	North	East	South
♥ Q J 10 9 8	pass	1♣	1♠	1NT
♦ 4 3 2				
♣ 10 6 4	Lead ♥Q, your own best suit.			
	You have ♠A as an entry.			

Partner doubles the final contract

♠ 9 6	West	North	East	South
♥ Q J 10 9 8		1♠	pass	1NT
♦ 4 3 2	pass	3NT	dble	all pass
♣ 10 6 4				

Partner's double is not like a double of an opening 1NT; it is asking for a specific lead of the suit bid by dummy. If dummy has bid two suits, it asks for a lead of the second suit. So lead ♠9, the only suit dummy bid – because partner told you to!

Partner doubles a conventional bid

♠ Q 9 6 3	West	North	East	South
♥ Q J 8 4	pass	pass	pass	1NT
♦ 4 3 2	pass	2♣	dble	2♦
♣ J 4	pass	2NT	all pass	

If opponents make a bid in a suit that they do not hold, you can double it to show the suit. A Stayman 2♣ bid or an ace showing response to Blackwood are examples of conventional bids. When partner is a passed hand, a double of 2♣ is showing clubs. Lead the ♣J. Be aware of these opportunities during the auction to help partner find the best lead.

Leading when there are few clues

Even the unhelpful auction of 1NT raised to 3NT has a few clues (they didn't seek a major suit fit, for example) but it is less informative than a more extensive auction.

If you lead your longest suit perhaps you will set up enough winners for your side, before declarer can cash nine tricks. So with:

♠ Q 10 8 6 5	Spades is your longest suit and the
♥ K 9 7 6	correct card to choose is the ♠6. Fourth
♦ 4 3	highest of your longest suit is right in
♣ K 6	this case and is very often the best lead
	for the defence.

Of course for the lead to succeed you need help from partner. Just one honour would be a great help.

Suppose partner has the jack. That would force out the ace or king and one more spade lead should set up three winners for you to cash.

```
                    ♠7 4
♠Q 10 8 6 5 [                ] ♠J 9 2
                    ♠A K 3
```

Give partner the ace or king and your winners may be set up straight away. There is a good chance that one of your club or heart kings will prove to be an entry so that you can cash those spade winners.

Sometimes declarer will have ♠A K J and you will give declarer a trick. Giving one trick doesn't necessarily mean giving the contract. Carry on with spades and two winners can still be set up.

Sometimes you can take your tricks straight away.

```
                    ♠K 7 6
♠Q 10 9 8 [                ] ♠A J 5 2
                    ♠4 3
```

The ten lead from an internal sequence is right. You lead ♠10, dummy and partner play low. Your ♠10 wins the trick. You play ♠9 and declarer cannot stop your side winning four spade tricks.

Choosing between two equal length suits

♠ Q 10 8 6
♥ K 8 6 5
♦ 4 3 2
♣ K 6

North   South
        1NT
3NT

A major looks a good lead, as they have not sought a major suit fit. But which one to choose? Look at spades. Any honour in partner's hand will help set up winners, whereas any heart honour will not. Lead the suit with the most honours. Note too that the heart is more likely to be an entry to cash your spade winners, than the spade would be to cash your hearts.


```
                    ♠9 5 3
    ♠Q 10 8 6   [            ]   ♠K 7 2
                    ♠A J 4
```

Lead ♠6, ♠3 from dummy, and ♠K from partner. If declarer wins the ♠A, you need to get partner in to lead through the ♠J 4, then you can take three spade tricks.

```
                    ♠9 5 3
    ♠Q 10 8 6   [            ]   ♠A 7 2
                    ♠K J 4
```

Lead ♠6. Partner wins ♠A and returns ♠7 (see page 26). Declarer can try playing ♠J but you can win and play a third spade setting up a spade winner to cash should you get in.

Leading with two equal length suits

■ Lead the suit with the most honours with two equal length suits.

■ If suits all have one honour, prefer to lead from a queen or king rather than an ace or a jack.

■ Look at the small cards. The 7, 8 and 9 are more useful than the 2, 3 and 4.

■ Lead the suit with a sequence of honours; if the number of honours is equal, e.g. lead from Q J 10 x rather than A Q 10 x.

■ Prefer an unbid major to an unbid minor.

When your suit is unsuitable

Sometimes your long suit is not a good one to lead, for example when an opponent has shown length in it.

♠ 9 6	North	South
♥ J 10 9 8 6	1♥	1NT
♦ 4 3 2	3NT	
♣ J 6 4		

Leading a heart must be wrong. If North has 4+ hearts, partner cannot have length in hearts. Your partner has values, probably ten or more points, so trying to lead partner's suit makes sense. You might lead a spade, saying 'No one has bid them, so partner must have spades'. But partner could easily have bid spades over 1♥ and yet failed to do so. Partner is more likely to have a minor – try ♣4, your better minor.

> When your suit won't do, lead your strongest 3-card suit.

♠ 9 6 2	North	South
♥ 6 5 4 3 2		1NT
♦ 4 3	3NT	
♣ J 6 4		

Your hearts are very weak and you have no outside entry. Leading hearts won't beat the contract. Partner could hold spades but be unable to bid them over 3NT, so a spade is probably the best choice. Lead ♠6.

♠ 9 6 2	North	South
♥ Q J 10 7 2		1NT
♦ 4 3	3NT	
♣ J 6 4		

With a very weak hand that has a good suit, lead that suit anyway. The lead may not do much good but it won't help declarer by giving away tricks. Leading ♥Q might just strike gold when the king is in dummy and partner has ♥A.

```
                    ♥K 3
    ♥Q J 10 7 2  [            ]  ♥A 9 5
                    ♥8 6 4
```

Leading a suit bid by opponents

This is a more advanced topic; you can omit this page if you want!

Occasionally the best lead is a suit bid by opponents, but you must have a good reason to make it. Partner will be short in the suit and not able to help you very much. For this reason it is often best to make a non-standard lead.

	North	South
♠ 9 6 2		
♥ Q J 10 9 6		1♥
♦ A 3	2♣	3NT
♣ Q J 10		

With a solid 4-card or 5-card sequence lead the ♥Q. But make the hearts weaker, ♥Q J 10 6 2, and it is right to lead ♥2. You need partner to produce one useful card. The ♥A or ♥K or even the ♥9 would do. Partner's honour might be a singleton. Don't waste two good cards on one trick, so lead a low card.

A non-standard lead is right even if it is dummy that bid the suit.

	North	South
♠ 9 6 2		
♥ Q J 10 6 2	1♥	2NT
♦ A 3	3NT	
♣ Q J 10		

Lead ♥2. Hope partner has ♥A, ♥K or ♥9, but maybe declarer will play the wrong card from dummy, not suspecting you would find such an unusual lead from a 5-card suit with three honours.

$$\begin{array}{c}
♥A 9 7 5 \\
♥Q J 10 6 2 \qquad\boxed{}\qquad ♥8 \\
♥K 4 3
\end{array}$$

Dummy will probably play the ♥5 and partner's ♥8 will force out the ♥K. Now if you gain the lead you can play on hearts to set up three winners. On the normal ♥Q lead, declarer can win the ♥K and still have two stoppers.

Think hard before you lead a suit bid by the declaring side.

Summary

- Lead partner's overcall suit. If it's worth a bid, it's worth a lead.

- The safest lead is the top card from a solid honour sequence. Prefer a 4-card suit with a good sequence to a weaker 5-card suit

- Fourth highest of your longest and strongest is often best.

- With two equal length suits, lead the one with more honours.

- Avoid leading suits bid by the opposition.

- To find partner's suit, try leading your strongest 3-card holding.

- If partner doubles 3NT unexpectedly, he is asking you to lead a suit bid by dummy.

- If partner doubles a conventional bid, it shows that suit.

Practise choosing the suit

The bidding is unhelpful. South opens 1NT, North bids 3NT. You are tossing up between two suits to lead, having nothing much in the other two suits. Which would you choose? Why?

Heart holding	Club holding	Lead
K Q J 10	K Q J 10	♥K. Prefer the major, but if the heart is ducked twice, you should certainly switch to clubs.
Q J 10 9	Q 6 5 4 2	♥Q. Despite five clubs the solid heart honours makes it favourite.
Q 4 3 2	Q 9 8 7	♥2 or ♣7. Those good club pips suggest clubs, but hearts is the unbid major. Very close.
A 6 4 3 2	K 7 6 4 3	♣4. Prefer to lead from a king. The ace is more likely to be an entry for your winners.
10 5 4 3 2	10 8 7 6 5	♣6. Club pips are better. With no entry maybe both could be wrong.

Quiz on leads against no trumps

West hand	Opponents bid	Your lead?
♠ 5 4 3 ♥ 8 6 ♦ K J 10 9 2 ♣ A 10 9	North South 1NT 3NT	♦J Top of an internal sequence.
♠ Q 10 8 7 4 ♥ 5 3 2 ♦ J 4 3 ♣ 10 3	North South 1♥ 1♠ 2♥ 3NT	♦3 You won't set up spades when South has bid them, so try the stronger minor.
♠ 6 4 ♥ Q J 10 8 7 ♦ 9 7 3 ♣ A 4 2	West North East South 1♠ 1NT all pass	♥Q Good 5-card suit and an entry, so lead your own suit.
♠ Q 9 7 5 3 ♥ 6 2 ♦ J 8 7 ♣ 6 5 3	North South 2NT 3♣ 3♥ 3NT	♦7 North has four spades. Partner could have doubled 3♣ for lead.
♠ 6 4 ♥ 8 6 5 3 ♦ K J 9 8 6 ♣ 10 2	West North East South 1♠ 1NT all pass	♠6 Lead partner's suit, as you have no entry to your own.
♠ Q J 10 9 ♥ 2 ♦ 6 5 4 3 ♣ 10 8 5 2	West North East South pass 1♥ pass 1NT pass 3NT dble all pass	♥2 This bidding asks for a heart lead. You have one, so lead it!

19

4 third hand play

Now move to the East seat and think what card you should play, when partner, West, makes the opening lead to 3NT.

Partner and dummy play small cards

Partner's small card lead usually shows 4+ cards with one or two honours.

If dummy has small cards, third hand plays high.

Playing a high card may not win the trick, but it will drive out declarer's stopper and start setting up winners for partner to cash.

If you have two or more touching high cards, play the lower one, e.g. jack from QJ. This can help partner work out what you hold.

If dummy has an honour you can beat, but that honour is not played, you may play a card that is not your highest one. For example:

	♠Q 6 2		
♠K 8 4 3	☐	♠A J 9	Play ♠J, and then declarer makes no spade tricks at all.
	♠10 7 5		

	♠Q 6 2		
♠K J 4 3	☐	♠A 10 5	Play ♠10, hoping partner has the jack.
	♠9 8 7		

	♠Q 6 2		
♠J 9 4 3	☐	♠A 10 5	Play ♠10. When declarer has ♠K he only makes one trick.
	♠K 8 7		

	♠Q 6 2		
♠10 8 4 3	☐	♠K 9 5	Play ♠9 and stop declarer making three spade tricks.
	♠A J 7		

When dummy has an honour you can beat, but it is not played, play your second highest card if it is a nine or better.

20

Practise your third hand play

Dummy has
♥Q 5 3

Partner
leads ♥4

Your play when you hold
1) ♥K 10 2
2) ♥A J 7
3) ♥A J 10
4) ♥K 8 7
5) ♥K 9 7

Dummy has
♥10 5 3

Partner
leads ♥4

Your play when you hold
6) ♥K 7 2
7) ♥A 9 7
8) ♥J 9 8
9) ♥K Q 2
10) ♥K J 7 2

Answers to the quiz

1) ♥10 if dummy plays low. But ♥K if ♥Q is played.

2) ♥J if dummy plays low. ♥A if ♥Q is played.

3) ♥10 if dummy plays low, play the lower of two touching cards.

4) ♥K. Only finesse against dummy if you hold the nine or better.

5) ♥9. Finesse with ♥9. Trust us, this works best.

6) ♥K. Third hand plays high when dummy has nothing.

7) ♥A. Third hand plays high when dummy has nothing.

8) ♥8. The lowest of touching cards, since ♥10 is in dummy.

9) ♥Q. The lower of two touching cards.

10) ♥K. Third hand high. Never play ♥J – to do so is finessing against partner. It may allow declarer's queen to win an unnecessary trick.

When partner leads an honour card

If partner leads a high honour, or the lead is won in dummy, so that you cannot beat the cards already played, tell partner what you think of his lead by the card you play. This is called an attitude signal.

When partner leads an honour, play a high card if you like the lead and a low card if you don't.

Third hand play when an honour is led

Suppose partner leads ♦Q. What sort of holding has partner?

The lead shows a solid or semi-solid sequence of diamonds headed by the ♦Q, either ♦Q J 10 x or ♦Q J 9 x. It might be a suit headed by ♦A Q J with small cards. Partner will usually have four or more diamonds but might lead a 3-card suit if it is ♦Q J 10. With ♦Q J x x, partner would lead fourth highest not the ♦Q.

Suppose there are three small cards in dummy. Do you like this lead? What card can you play to tell partner what you hold?

If you hold the ace, win the trick and return the suit.

If you have ♦K and three or more cards, play the highest of your small cards to encourage partner to continue the lead.

If you have the king but it is doubleton you should play the king to get out of partner's way – it won't always be right but it is the best play in the long run. If you don't unblock, declarer can win the ♦A. Then when you get in, you can cash the ♦K but have no more diamonds left to put partner on lead. If dummy has ♦A and it is played, you must still unblock your ♦K.

If you have ♦10, play an encouraging card from three or four. The ten is a useful card when partner has the ♦Q and ♦J.

Without any honour and only two or three cards, play your smallest card to show no interest.

The Rule of Eleven

When partner leads a fourth highest card, the Rule of Eleven helps work out who has what. It may sound complicated but give it a try. For example, partner leads the 6. The A K Q J 10 9 8 7 are all higher than the 6. Partner has three of these, so the remaining five cards must be in the other three hands.

Subtract the value of the card led from eleven. This gives the number of cards bigger than that led in the remaining hands.

Count how many you and dummy hold. The cards left must be in declarer's hand.

Partner leads ♠7, dummy plays ♠3. What should you play?

♠Q 8 5 3

♠7 led ━━━━━━━━ ♠K 10 6

Use the Rule of Eleven.

■ Subtract 7 from 11 giving the answer 4.

■ Count how many cards you can see higher than the seven

■ Dummy has two, so do you. This means declarer has no cards higher than the seven. The position must be:

♠Q 8 5 3

♠A J 9 7 ━━━━━━━━ ♠K 10 6

♠4 2

If declarer plays dummy's ♠3, play your ♠6, and partner can make another lead through dummy's ♠Q.

Should the ♠7 lose to the ♠A, you know partner has not led fourth highest. Maybe partner was trying to find your suit.

♠A J 7

♠6 led ━━━━━━━━ ♠K 9 4

The ♠6 is covered by ♠7. Which card do you play?

Work it out. 11–6 = 5. You can see five cards higher than the six, so declarer has none. You should play ♠9 not ♠K, expecting this to hold the trick. Partner has ♠Q 10 8 6 5. Now return the ♠K to set up winners for partner.

When the lead is won in dummy

When partner's opening lead is won in dummy, a high card from you says you want to encourage the lead. A low card shows no interest.

Say partner leads ♦2 and declarer plays ♦A from dummy's ♦A 6 4 holding. You have ♦Q 8 3. Play ♦8 to encourage partner.

You should mildly encourage with any 4-card holding. So play ♦5 from ♦9 8 5 3. But from two or three small cards play your smallest card to let partner know you can provide no help here.

When not to play high in third seat

This is a more advanced topic; you can omit this section if you want!

This is harder to find at the table, but easier seeing all four hands.

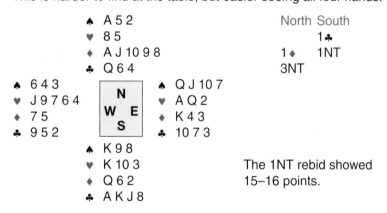

	♠ A 5 2	North	South
	♥ 8 5		1♣
	♦ A J 10 9 8	1♦	1NT
	♣ Q 6 4	3NT	

♠ 6 4 3   ♠ Q J 10 7
♥ J 9 7 6 4   ♥ A Q 2
♦ 7 5   ♦ K 4 3
♣ 9 5 2   ♣ 10 7 3

    ♠ K 9 8
    ♥ K 10 3   The 1NT rebid showed
    ♦ Q 6 2   15–16 points.
    ♣ A K J 8

West leads ♥6. How should you, as East, plan the defence? Dummy has 11 points, you have 12, declarer 15 or 16, leaving West with only 1 or 2 points. You win ♥A, play ♥Q, but declarer does not win his ♥K until the third round, leaving partner with two winners but no entry.

Declarer doesn't know who has ♥A or ♦K. Play ♥Q at trick one. Declarer must win ♥K. When you win ♦K, you cash ♥A and play another heart to partner's ♥J to get the contract one down.

With fewer points, you play the cards normally, i.e. ♥A then ♥Q.

Returning partner's lead

If you win trick one, or if you get the lead at a later trick, it is normal to

return partner's lead when you get in.

You may have a suit you wish partner had led, but don't switch suits unless you have a very good reason. Look at this example

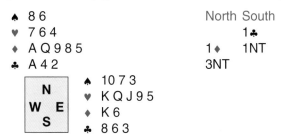

```
    ♠ 8 6              North South
    ♥ 7 6 4                     1♣
    ♦ A Q 9 8 5        1♦      1NT
    ♣ A 4 2            3NT
              ♠ 10 7 3
        N     ♥ K Q J 9 5
      W   E   ♦ K 6
        S     ♣ 8 6 3
```

Partner leads ♠5 and your ♠10 forces out declarer's ♠J. Declarer plays ♦J to your king. Do you now play ♠7 or ♥K?

Yes, of course you wish partner had led a heart (did you overcall?) but that chance has gone and so has your entry. Don't waste time on regrets.

Rule of Eleven says 11−5 = 6 and you can see four cards higher than the five, so declarer has two cards one of which was ♠J. Return a spade and you will find partner cashing four spade tricks for one down. The complete deal was:

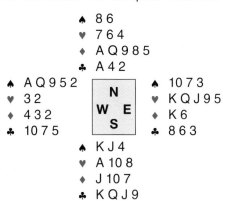

```
                ♠ 8 6
                ♥ 7 6 4
                ♦ A Q 9 8 5
                ♣ A 4 2
   ♠ A Q 9 5 2              ♠ 10 7 3
   ♥ 3 2          N         ♥ K Q J 9 5
   ♦ 4 3 2      W   E       ♦ K 6
   ♣ 10 7 5        S        ♣ 8 6 3
                ♠ K J 4
                ♥ A 10 8
                ♦ J 10 7
                ♣ K Q J 9
```

Which card to lead back

The card you play back tells partner how many cards you hold.

- If you started with two cards you have no choice.
- If you started with three cards, return your higher card.
- If you started with four cards, return the original fourth highest.
- With an honour sequence, return the highest honour.

You hold	Play
♣Q 9 3	Win with ♣Q. Play back ♣9.
♣K 2	Win with ♣K. Play back ♣2.
♣K 7 5 3	Win with ♣K. Play back ♣3.
♣K 8 7 5 3	Win with ♣K. Play back ♣5.
♣K Q 7	Win with ♣Q. Play back ♣K.
♣K Q 7 5	Win with ♣Q. Play back ♣5.
♣Q J 10	Win with ♣10. Play back ♣Q.

This hand shows why it matters which card you play back.

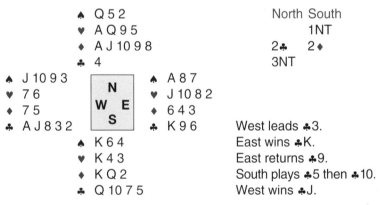

♠ Q 5 2
♥ A Q 9 5
♦ A J 10 9 8
♣ 4

♠ J 10 9 3
♥ 7 6
♦ 7 5
♣ A J 8 3 2

♠ A 8 7
♥ J 10 8 2
♦ 6 4 3
♣ K 9 6

♠ K 6 4
♥ K 4 3
♦ K Q 2
♣ Q 10 7 5

North	South
	1NT
2♣	2♦
3NT	

West leads ♣3.
East wins ♣K.
East returns ♣9.
South plays ♣5 then ♣10.
West wins ♣J.

The ♣K denies ♣Q and ♣9 shows East has only two or three clubs. So South has at least four clubs including ♣Q. The queen won't drop under ♣A. West must try to get East on lead to play another club. Switch to ♠J.

When not to return partner's lead

If you win trick one, it is normal to return the suit partner led. But normal does not mean always. Look at this hand.

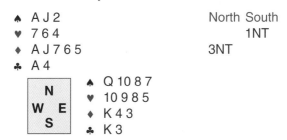

♠ A J 2	North South
♥ 7 6 4	1NT
♦ A J 7 6 5	3NT
♣ A 4	

Partner leads ♣5, declarer plays low from dummy and you win the ♣K. Do you return a club? First of all watch what declarer plays to the first trick. If it is ♣2 you know partner has led a 4-card club suit. That means South has five clubs, so by returning a club you are setting up declarer's long suit. Declarer won't have a 4-card major as well as five clubs, so partner must have at least three in each major. This is the time to switch. Lead up to weakness in dummy and switch to ♥10.

Summary

■ Third hand plays high with small cards in dummy.

■ When dummy has an honour you can beat, finesse against it with the nine or higher. If you hold no other card higher than the nine, play your honour.

■ With two or more touching cards, play the lower of the two.

■ Unless you have a very good reason not to, return partner's lead.

■ Return the higher card from three but the original fourth highest from four or more.

■ Tell partner your attitude to his lead: a high card to encourage.

■ If the lead against no trumps is a king, unblock any honour you hold. Without an honour give a count signal (high-low = even number).

■ The Rule of Eleven helps place the high cards on a low card lead.

Practise working out the distribution

Get a pack of cards and just use the diamond suit.

The table below shows partner's lead and dummy's cards in a 3NT contract. The card dummy played is underlined.

Pick out the cards you can see. Those that are left must either be in partner's or declarer's hand. In the first example you can see ♦A K Q 9 7 6 5 leaving ♦J 10 8 4 3 2. Work out how those cards are placed, e.g. partner might have ♦Q J 10 2, leaving declarer with ♦8 4 3.

Decide what message you want to send partner and which card in your hand will carry that message. Check that this works out well.

Partner's Lead	Dummy holds	You hold	Your action Make up your mind first!
♦Q	♦K 6 <u>5</u>	♦A 9 7	If dummy plays ♦5, play ♦9 to encourage a continuation.
♦Q	♦<u>K</u> 6 5	♦A 9 7 or ♦A 9	If dummy plays ♦K, win your ♦A and return ♦9.
♦Q	♦6 5 <u>2</u>	♦A 9 7	Win your ♦A and return ♦9.
♦Q	♦5 <u>2</u>	♦K 9 7 3	Play ♦9, to encourage.
♦Q	♦5 <u>2</u>	♦A 9 7 3	Win ♦A, return ♦3, to show you started with four diamonds.
♦Q	♦6 5 <u>2</u>	♦K 9	Play ♦K to unblock the suit. Return ♦9, if the ♦K wins.
♦Q	♦<u>A</u> 5 2	♦K 9	Play ♦K to unblock whether or not ♦A is played.
♦Q	♦6 5 <u>2</u>	♦7 4 3 or ♦4 3	Play ♦3 to show two or three small cards and no honours.

Practise returning partner's lead

West leads the ♦5. What do you play to trick one? If that card wins what do you play to trick two? Would you switch to another suit?

Dummy	You hold	Trick 1?	Trick 2?
♦4 3 <u>2</u>	♦K 8 7 6	♦K	♦6, this shows an original 4-card holding.
♦4 3 <u>2</u>	♦K 8 7	♦K	♦8, this shows two or three cards.
♦4 <u>3</u>	♦K Q J 6	♦J	♦K, this shows either KQJ alone or KQJx. Play back ♦K to unblock in case partner has five cards.
♦4 <u>3</u>	♦K J 7 6 2	♦K	♦6, show a 4+ card holding.
♦Q 4 <u>3</u>	♦A J 7	♦J	♦A, West has ♦K as your ♦J held the trick.
♦Q 4 <u>3</u>	♦K 10 7	♦10	♦K, West has ♦A and ♦J if your ♦10 wins the trick.
♦4 <u>3</u>	♦A K 6 2	♦K	West may have Jxxx. Lead ♦2 and give declarer a guess.
♦4 3 <u>2</u>	♦A Q 7	♦A	♦Q to set up or cash winners in diamonds.
♦A 3 <u>2</u>	♦K Q 6	♦Q	♦K to unblock the suit.
♦A <u>2</u>	♦K Q 6	♦Q	♦K. If you play ♦6 you might block the suit.
♦A Q <u>2</u>	♦K J 6	♦J	Play another suit – get partner in to lead another diamond.
♦4 <u>2</u>	♦K 3	♦K	Switch to something else. Declarer has five diamonds.

5 opening leader's next play

Let's return to the West seat. You have made your opening lead and seen what cards were played to the first trick. What can you deduce from those cards?

```
                    ♠6 2
♠J 8 5 4 3    [============]    ♠10 played
                    ♠K played
```

You lead ♠4, partner plays the ♠10. Where are the rest of the spades?

Third player plays high. This means East will do the best he can to win the trick, so there is no way East has either the ace or the queen. You have seen the king and you have the jack. The ten is East's best spade. East can't have the ♠9, it would be played rather than the ♠10, since WE play the lower of touching cards. So South has ♠9.

You now know South had exactly ♠A K Q 9 and East had ♠10 7. This places nine of South's points. It's amazing how one card can say so much. You would be wasting your time if you continued spades next time you are on lead.

```
                    ♠6 2
♠K 9 4 3      [============]    ♠J played
                    ♠A played
```

You lead the ♠3. Who has ♠10? Who has ♠Q?

Partner has the ♠Q. Declarer would have won with the ♠Q if he had it. Declarer has ♠10; partner would play ♠10 in preference to ♠J.

```
                    ♠A 6 2
♠K 8 5 4 3    [============]    ♠J played
                    ♠Q played
```

You lead ♠4. Who has ♠10?

South has ♠Q 10 (x) (x); another spade from you gives a trick away.

When to duck the second trick

You lead ♥6 against 3NT. When dummy goes down you can see:

		North	South
♠	A 5 2		1♣
♥	10 5		
♦	A J 10 9 8 6	1♦	1NT
♣	Q 4	3NT	

```
              N
♠ 6 4 3
♥ K 9 7 6 4   W   E
♦ 7 5
♣ 9 5 2       S
```

Partner wins ♥A and returns ♥8. Declarer plays ♥2 to trick one and ♥Q to trick two. Should you win your ♥K?

If partner started with ♥J, he would have led it back instead of ♥8. So don't be fooled by declarer's ♥Q, he has ♥J hidden in his hand. It is most likely that South started with ♥Q J 2. He did not rebid 1♥ over 1♦, so he won't have four hearts. Partner has ♥A 8 3.

Duck the second round of your suit, as you haven't an entry.

The king is your only entry to the two potential heart winners. Hope partner gets in to play his ♥3. Follow with ♥4 to show you started with five hearts.

Now suppose something slightly different happens.

You lead ♥6 and trick one goes the same way. But at trick two partner returns ♥3 and declarer plays ♥Q. Look carefully at those heart pips. The three is partner's lowest heart. He either started with ♥A J 8 3 or ♥A 3. In either case, win your king and play back ♥4. If partner had only two hearts there is nothing you can do, but if partner had four hearts declarer started with two, ♥Q 2 and you can win five heart tricks straightaway to beat the contract. This hand illustrates why it is so important to agree which card East should return.

East returns his highest card if he started with two or three, but his original fourth highest if he started with four or more.

This is nearly the same position.

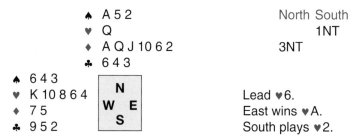

```
        ♠ A 5 2                  North South
        ♥ Q 10                            1♣
        ♦ A J 10 9 8 6            1♦     1NT
        ♣ 6 4                     3NT
♠ 6 4 3        ┌──────┐
♥ K 9 7 6 4    │   N   │
♦ 7 5          │ W   E │
♣ 9 5 2        │   S   │
               └──────┘
```

Again you lead ♥6. The ♥10 is played from dummy, partner wins trick one with ♥A and declarer plays ♥2. Partner returns ♥8 and declarer plays ♥3. Do you let dummy's ♥Q win the trick?

It is the same problem, whether North or South holds ♥Q. The key point is still that partner does not hold ♥J. With ♥Q in dummy, partner would have played ♥J at trick one if holding ♥A J 8. Duck the trick and hope that partner can win a trick and has another heart to play.

This deal looks the same but there are subtle differences.

```
        ♠ A 5 2                  North South
        ♥ Q                               1NT
        ♦ A Q J 10 6 2           3NT
        ♣ 6 4 3
♠ 6 4 3        ┌──────┐
♥ K 10 8 6 4   │   N   │        Lead ♥6.
♦ 7 5          │ W   E │        East wins ♥A.
♣ 9 5 2        │   S   │        South plays ♥2.
               └──────┘
```

East returns ♥7 and declarer plays ♥9. You win ♥10. What now?

East can only have three hearts on ♥7 return, so South has four. Something like ♥J 9 5 2. Cashing ♥K will not beat the contract as South still has a stopper with ♥J. You must get partner in to lead another heart. Switch to a spade and hope partner has an entry.

If partner had returned ♥3 you would win ♥10 and continue with ♥K, confidently expecting partner to have started with ♥A 7 5 3.

For a good defence, it is important to notice partner's signals and vital that you can trust them.

When to switch

```
        ♠ K 2              North  South
        ♥ 10 5             2♦     3♣
        ♦ A K Q 9 8 6 3    3♦     3NT
        ♣ A 4
♠ Q J 3
♥ A 9 7 6 4    
♦ 7 5          
♣ 9 5 2        
```

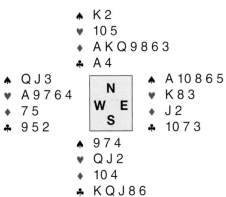

Whether North opens 1♦ or 2♦, opponents arrive in 3NT. You lead ♥6. Partner wins ♥K and returns ♥8. Declarer plays the ♥2 to trick one and ♥J to trick two. Declarer must have the ♥Q, as partner played ♥K at trick one. Do you win the second trick or do you duck ♥J to keep your entry?

If you don't win, declarer must make one heart, one club and seven diamonds – the nine tricks needed. Win ♥K and switch to ♠Q. To beat this contract WE must win five tricks quickly. Spades are our only hope. Just hope those spades include ♠A and ♠10.

The complete deal was:

```
                ♠ K 2
                ♥ 10 5
                ♦ A K Q 9 8 6 3
                ♣ A 4
♠ Q J 3              N        ♠ A 10 8 6 5
♥ A 9 7 6 4      W       E    ♥ K 8 3
♦ 7 5                S        ♦ J 2
♣ 9 5 2                       ♣ 10 7 3
                ♠ 9 7 4
                ♥ Q J 2
                ♦ 10 4
                ♣ K Q J 8 6
```

If you duck the second heart, declarer makes twelve tricks.

Showing your entry

South opens 1NT and everybody passes. Let's look at this problem from the East seat first. West leads out the ♣K ♣Q and ♣J. You follow twice and discard a diamond on the third round. Declarer wins the ♣A and leads ♦Q. You win your king. What should you play now? A spade looks safest. A heart could so easily give declarer a trick.

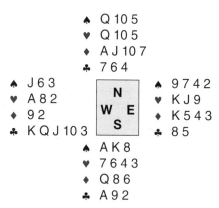

```
        ♠  Q 10 5
        ♥  Q 10 5
        ♦  A J 10 7
        ♣  7 6 4
                      ♠  9 7 4 2
              N       ♥  K J 9
          W       E   ♦  K 5 4 3
              S       ♣  8 5
```

Look at the deal from the West seat. You lead ♣K, it wins, and partner plays ♣8. You lead ♣Q that wins, partner plays ♣5. You know partner doesn't have ♣A, the king lead told him to unblock at trick one.

```
                ♠  Q 10 5
                ♥  Q 10 5
                ♦  A J 10 7
                ♣  7 6 4
  ♠  J 6 3                       ♠  9 7 4 2
  ♥  A 8 2         N             ♥  K J 9
  ♦  9 2       W       E         ♦  K 5 4 3
  ♣  K Q J 10 3     S            ♣  8 5
                ♠  A K 8
                ♥  7 6 4 3
                ♦  Q 8 6
                ♣  A 9 2
```

The only club left is declarer's ♣A. You can lead any of your clubs to drive it out. You know you can get in with ♥A to cash your clubs but partner doesn't. How can you tell him?

Looking at dummy your entry won't be in diamonds, but how can partner choose between spades and hearts?

The answer lies in the card you lead to set up the clubs. To lead the highest club would ask for a spade, the higher card asks for the higher-ranking suit. To lead the ♣3, the lowest outstanding club, would ask for a heart. East can see for himself that you cannot want a diamond. This is called a suit preference signal. This useful signal will turn up in a number of places but the idea is always the same.

When you have a choice of cards you can lead, send a signal with the card you choose. So ♣3 asks for a heart and ♣J for a spade.

A high card asks for the higher ranking suit.
A low card asks for the lower ranking suit.

Here is another example:

		West	North	East	South
♠	K 5 3				1♣
♥	10 7 2				
♦	A Q 10 9 8 6	1♥	2♦	pass	3NT
♣	6	all pass			

♠ A 6
♥ K J 9 6 4 3
♦ 5
♣ 9 5 4 2

You lead ♥6.
Partner plays ♥Q. It wins. East returns ♥5.

South played ♥8 to trick one and ♥A to trick two. What card should you play to trick two?

You must hope that partner can win a diamond trick or the contract is very likely to make. When partner wins, you want a spade lead so that you can cash all those heart winners. Play the ♥K under the ace. It can't cost a trick, dummy's ♥10 is the only other heart left out and you have ♥J.

That ♥K should grab partner's attention and tell him you want a spade lead. What else could it mean? Swap your black suits round and you would play ♥3 to ask partner to lead a club.

When you can play any card in the suit without giving away a trick, give a suit preference signal.

Make your signals as clear as you safely can. Give partner a slap, not a tickle.

Switching to another suit

Sometimes you have to switch your attack to another suit to defeat the contract. Look at this deal:

		North	South
♠ 6 4			1NT
♥ J 6 4			
♦ A K Q J		2NT	3NT
♣ J 8 5 4			

♠ Q 9 7 5 2
♥ K 3 2
♦ 10 9
♣ A K 6

```
    N
W       E
    S
```

You lead ♠5.
Partner plays ♠J.
Declarer wins ♠A.

Declarer crosses to dummy with a diamond, partner playing the ♦2, and leads the ♥J running it to your ♥K. What now?

Partner's play of ♠J denies both ♠10 and ♠K, declarer must have started with ♠A K 10, and so he still has ♠K 10 in hand. Leading a spade would give a cheap trick to ♠10. Declarer has four diamond tricks and the heart play will have set up three tricks in hearts as the suit breaks 3-3. If we can beat the contract it has to be with clubs.

Lead ♣A. You hope partner will give an encouraging signal by playing a high card. Continue with ♣K and ♣5. Partner started with just enough to get the contract one down.

♠ J 8 3
♥ 9 8 5
♦ 7 3 2
♣ Q 10 6 2

Partner had to have four clubs including ♣Q. The ten was not absolutely necessary: ♣Q 9 x x would have been good enough. Put out the cards and check that statement.

Your ♣A K 5 made it easier to switch to clubs, but you must find that switch even with unattractive holdings, such as ♣A Q 5 or ♣K Q 5.

Don't automatically continue leading your long suit.

Stop and think how many tricks declarer can make.

Here is another position where it can be right to switch to another suit.

```
          ♠ Q 10 5
          ♥ Q 10 5
          ♦ A J 10 7
          ♣ 7 6 4
♠ J 6 3      ┌─────────┐
♥ 9 8 2      │    N    │
♦ 9 2        │ W     E │
♣ K Q J 10 3 │    S    │
             └─────────┘
```

You saw a similar West hand a few pages ago. The difference is that this time you don't have an ace, so if you set up your clubs you can't get in to cash the winners. If declarer ducks two club tricks, you should switch to either a heart or a spade. It's a guess which, but ♥9 looks best. On a really good day partner will have ♥A K J x.

Summary

■ A partnership has agreements about which card should be played in a particular situation. Often it will seem irrelevant which card you play, but you never know when a signal will help partner, so stick to the agreement.

■ When both partners play those agreed cards, a great deal of information can be deduced.

■ Without an outside entry, it can be correct to duck when partner returns your suit.

■ Use suit preference signals to show where your entry lies.

■ Using suit preference you play the highest card you can spare to ask for the higher ranking suit and the lowest card to ask for the lower ranking suit.

■ Don't automatically keep playing the suit that was first led. Sometimes it is right to switch, particularly if you don't have an entry to cash your winners.

Practise your card reading

South opened 1NT and all passed. From the cards played work out what South might hold.

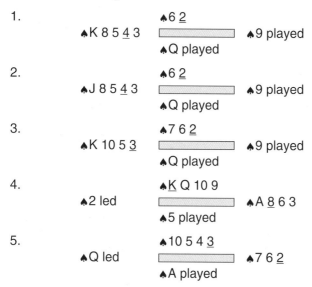

1.
              ♠6 2
♠K 8 5 <u>4</u> 3   ♠9 played
              ♠Q played

2.
              ♠6 2
♠J 8 5 <u>4</u> 3   ♠9 played
              ♠Q played

3.
              ♠7 6 <u>2</u>
♠K 10 5 <u>3</u>   ♠9 played
              ♠Q played

4.
              ♠<u>K</u> Q 10 9
♠2 led   ♠A <u>8</u> 6 3
              ♠5 played

5.
              ♠10 5 4 <u>3</u>
♠Q led   ♠7 6 <u>2</u>
              ♠A played

1. South has ♠A Q, ♠A Q J, ♠A Q 7 or maybe ♠A Q J 7. Partner has either ♠J 10 9, ♠10 9 or just ♠9. If declarer has ♠10 then he must have ♠J as well since East would play ♠J from ♠J 9 x.

2. South would normally win the trick with the ten if he held it. So partner has ♠10 9 and declarer ♠A K Q.

3. As you hold ♠10, you know ♠9 is partner's highest spade. He would have played higher if he could. South must have A Q J 8.

4. If ♠2 is fourth highest, ♠5 is South's only spade. As South opened 1NT this is unlikely. Work out why partner led from ♠J x x.

5. South has ♠A K since partner's ♠Q denied the ♠K. Probably partner has ♠Q J 9 8 and South has ♠A K alone.

6 second hand play

On many deals declarer wins the suit led and starts to set up his tricks. There are some general principles to guide how you should play when declarer leads from his hand towards dummy or from dummy towards his hand.

General rule, often true – second hand plays low.

Like all generalities, it is not always true. When an opponent leads to a trick, your side is last to play to the trick – so partner has a chance to beat a high card from dummy. For example:

```
              ♦Q 6 3
♦K 9 4      [          ]      ♦A 10 5
              ♦J 8 7 2
```

The ♦2 is led. If you play low your side must take three tricks. Put out the cards to check this. But if you play your ♦K on ♦2, declarer can set up a second diamond winner. This suit is nearly the same:

```
              ♦K 6 3
♦A 9 3      [          ]      ♦J 10 5
              ♦Q 8 7 2
```

Holding ♦K and ♦Q, declarer must make one trick. When ♦2 is led, don't play ♦A or declarer makes three diamonds. Play low, let ♦K win. When partner plays ♦10 to the next trick, declarer can play low and let ♦10 win or play ♦Q losing to ♦A leaving ♦J a winner.

```
              ♦K Q 7 4
♦A J 9      [          ]      ♦10 5 3
              ♦8 6 2
```

Declarer leads ♦2. Don't leap up with ♦A. It helps declarer make three diamond tricks. Play low. Declarer needs to return to his hand to lead another diamond and he can't be sure your partner doesn't hold ♦A. Partner might well duck the first time when holding ♦A. Declarer may give up on this suit, which is lying favourably, and look elsewhere for tricks.

Keep your honours to beat the opponents' honours.

On the previous examples it was clear which card would be played from dummy. Sometimes declarer has to make a guess.

```
                  ♦K J 9 4
   ♦A 5 3      [            ]      ♦Q 10 7
                  ♦8 6 2
```

Play low when ♦2 is led: declarer might play ♦J losing to ♦Q. Play low again if ♦6 is led: declarer might finesse ♦9 this time. You must play low smoothly – in tempo, as it is called. If you think for ages and then produce ♦3, declarer may guess your holding.

When to play high as second in hand

Of course, there are times when second hand does not play low. The most usual is when declarer leads an honour, for example:

```
                  ♦A Q 7
   ♦K 4 2      [            ]      ♦10 9 8 3
                  ♦J 6 5
```

♦J is led. You must play your ♦K. If you don't, declarer will play low from dummy and make three diamond tricks. If you cover ♦J, partner's ♦10 wins the third round. Some declarers wrongly think the following is a finesse. When ♦Q is led, it will win if you fail to cover with ♦K.

```
                  ♦A 9 7 4
   ♦K 8 5      [            ]      ♦J 10 3
                  ♦Q 6 2
```

Cover an honour with an honour.

Suppose you are East and dummy leads ♦Q. When there are two touching honours in dummy, cover the second one not the first.

```
                  ♦Q J 9
   ♦10 4 3     [            ]      ♦K 8 5
                  ♦A 7 6 2
```

♦Q is led. You play ♦5. ♦Q wins the trick and ♦J is led. This time you cover with ♦K and promote a trick for partner's ♦10. If you cover the first time, declarer could finesse ♦9 on the way back.

Consider this suit, when declarer leads ♦6.

```
                    ♦A 9 4 2
♦Q J 10 8      [            ]      ♦5 3
                    ♦K 7 6
```

It is just possible that declarer is planning to duck a diamond and you would hate ♦9 to win. Follow suit with ♦10, the lowest card in the sequence, to tell partner about your diamonds.

Lead the highest honour of a sequence, but play the lowest of the sequence when following suit.

Win your honour, if you can cash enough tricks to beat the contract.

```
                    ♦Q 10 7 4
♦K 8 5         [            ]      ♦J 9 3
                    ♦A 6 2
```

Declarer plays ♦2. If you only had ♦K 8 this would be easy, you would rise with ♦K. But normally with ♦K 8 5 you would play low, leaving declarer with a guess which card to play from dummy. However, if you have four winners set up, play your king and cash them. You might not get a second chance.

Cover an honour with an honour is a good generalisation but there are occasions when it is wrong.

```
                    ♦A 3
♦K 8 5         [            ]      ♦?
                    ♦Q led
```

Play low on ♦Q and your ♦K must score a trick eventually.

```
                    ♦A J 10 9 8 7
♦K 6 5 2       [            ]      ♦?
                    ♦Q led
```

Play low on ♦Q. There are no winners to be set up by covering. If declarer has only one or two diamonds, a trick will have to be lost to your king. It is always true that if you can see all the missing high cards there is no point in covering an honour. We cover to promote our side's lesser cards into taking tricks. If that cannot happen, don't cover.

Second hand high to stop dummy's suit

This is a more advanced topic; you can omit this section if you want!

Second hand high sometimes stops dummy's long suit being set up.

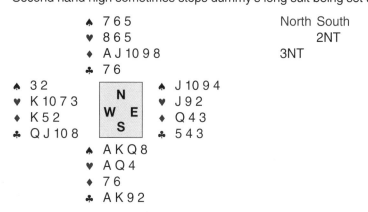

```
              ♠ 7 6 5              North  South
              ♥ 8 6 5                     2NT
              ♦ A J 10 9 8          3NT
              ♣ 7 6
  ♠ 3 2          N         ♠ J 10 9 4
  ♥ K 10 7 3   W   E       ♥ J 9 2
  ♦ K 5 2        S         ♦ Q 4 3
  ♣ Q J 10 8               ♣ 5 4 3
              ♠ A K Q 8
              ♥ A Q 4
              ♦ 7 6
              ♣ A K 9 2
```

You are West and lead ♣Q. South has three spades, one heart, one diamond and two clubs – only seven tricks. A 3-3 spade break and a winning heart finesse would make nine. But it's less than a 20% chance; playing diamonds is better odds.

South leads a diamond and plays dummy's ♦8. If East wins ♦Q, a second finesse brings home the suit. East can duck ♦Q and now declarer has two diamond tricks. Can you do better?

Look what happens if you play ♦K at trick two. If the ace is taken that is the last diamond declarer wins. If declarer ducks ♦K, playing for you to hold ♦K Q and finesses on the next round, declarer makes no diamonds at all. Declarer is fixed by your ♦K play and must go down.

Get your cards and put out just the diamond suit.

```
                    ♦A J 10 9 8
        ♦K 5 2      [            ]    ♦Q 4 3
                    ♦7 6
```

Play this suit, first when West plays low on the first round and second when West plays high. Now give West ♦K Q 2 and you will see that West does best to play LOW on the first round, letting declarer make two diamond tricks but not four.

Second hand high to gain an entry

This is a more advanced topic; you can omit this section if you want!

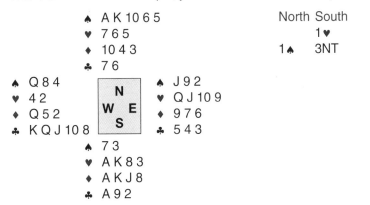

```
              ♠ A K 10 6 5              North  South
              ♥ 7 6 5                           1♥
              ♦ 10 4 3                    1♠     3NT
              ♣ 7 6
♠ Q 8 4          N          ♠ J 9 2
♥ 4 2         W     E        ♥ Q J 10 9
♦ Q 5 2          S          ♦ 9 7 6
♣ K Q J 10 8                ♣ 5 4 3
              ♠ 7 3
              ♥ A K 8 3
              ♦ A K J 8
              ♣ A 9 2
```

Naturally, you lead ♣K and ♣Q, both of which hold. To trick three you lead ♣8. You play ♣8 to suggest your entry is in diamonds rather than hearts (see page 34). South leads ♠3, playing ♠10 from dummy. Partner wins and switches to a diamond, as your signal suggested. The ♦A wins and South makes four spades, two hearts, two diamonds and a club.

You could do better. Play ♠Q on the first round of spades and declarer cannot make 3NT. Either he lets ♠Q win so that you can cash your clubs, or he takes ♠Q and concedes a spade to partner and then has no entry to dummy's spades.

Summary

- Normally second hand plays low when a small card is led, but if you can cash enough winners to beat the contract, play high!

- If an honour is led, second hand covers the honour in the hope of making our side's smaller cards into winners.

- Don't cover an honour if all the cards that might become winners are in dummy.

- Cover the second of two touching honours.

- Play the lowest when following with a sequence of honours.

Practise second hand play

Declarer leads and you must play second. Which card do you play?

Lead	You hold	Dummy	Answer
♦Q	♦K 5	♦A J 9 6	♦K. Hope partner has ♦10.
♦10	♦K 5	♦A J 9 6	♦K. Hope partner has ♦Q 8 x x.
♦Q	♦K 4 3 2	♦AJ1098	♦2. There is nothing to promote.
♦8	♦K 5	♦A 9 6 4	♦5. Don't waste your king.
♦2	♦K Q J 3	♦A 9 6 4	♦J. Play the lowest card of a sequence.
♦3	♦K 7 5	♦Q 10 8	♦5. Declarer may have to guess whether to play ♦Q or ♦10 from dummy.
♦3	♦K 10 5	♦Q 4 2	♦5. Best play, partner may have Axx
♦Q	♦K 7 5	♦A 4 2	♦5. If declarer is a good player, assume he has ♦J and cover the next honour. Else cover ♦Q!

Dummy leads (so you can see what cards dummy holds). You are second to play. Which card do you play?

Dummy	You Hold	Answer
♦Q J 9 8	♦K 7 6	♦6. Cover ♦J next time.
♦J 8 5 4	♦K 7 6 3 2	♦2. Too many diamonds in sight to cover.
♦J 8 5 4	♦K 10	♦K. If declarer has shown a 6-card suit, you should play the 10; partner might have singleton A!
♦Q 2	♦A K 8	♦K. Occasionally you might duck, if you suspect declarer has a long suit.

7 count signals

The best way to beat a contract is to build up a picture of the hands you cannot see. This picture of the unseen hands should include both the high cards and the distribution of the suits.

WE do not always beat the contract by cashing our tricks quickly. Sometimes declarer hasn't enough tricks unless WE help.

Count signals on declarer's suit

When partner leads an honour card or a suit where the trick is won in dummy, WE know that WE play signals that tell partner about our attitude to the lead. A high card encourages, a low card discourages.

However this type of signal is not very useful when declarer leads a suit. If WE like the suit, probably declarer won't be playing it!

On declarer's lead, it is far more useful to play count signals. Count signals were first introduced in Chapter 2, when looking at what to play when partner leads a king against a no trump contract. This Chapter looks at other uses of count signals.

In a suit led by declarer:
A high then a lower card shows an even number of cards.
A low then a higher card shows an odd number of cards.

So with a club holding of, say:

♣5 2	Play ♣5 first, then ♣2, to show two.
♣7 5 2	Play ♣2 first, followed by ♣5, to show three.
♣10 7 5 2	Play ♣7 first, then ♣2 to show four. Normally, play the second highest then the fourth highest.
♣10 8 7 5 2	Play ♣2 first, then ♣8, then ♣5 to show five cards.
♣10 8 7 5 3 2	Play ♣8, next ♣5, then ♣2 to show six.

Give this count signal any time it might be of use to your partner. But remember, declarer too can draw inferences from the cards you play.

Look at how useful a count signal is in this example:

♠ 5 3   North South
♥ 7 5 2   2NT
♦ 4 3 2   3NT
♣ K Q J 9 3

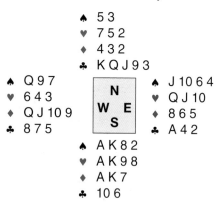

♠ J 10 6 4   West leads ♦Q.
♥ Q J 10   Declarer wins ♦A.
♦ 8 6 5   Declarer plays ♣10.
♣ A 4 2   How do you defend?

The defence can hold up too. You allow ♣10 to hold the trick.
Dummy has no entry outside the club suit. Don't play your ♣A
until declarer plays his last club or he will make four club tricks.
But how do you know when he plays his last club? You know
because partner tells you how many he has with a count signal.

When ♣10 holds, declarer plays ♣6 to dummy's jack. Do you win
this trick? Did declarer start with two or three clubs? Pay attention
to partner's signal. Did partner play ♣5 first? This is the lowest
outstanding club and so partner has an odd number of clubs,
which must be three. Now you win the second club.

                    ♠ 5 3
                    ♥ 7 5 2
                    ♦ 4 3 2
                    ♣ K Q J 9 3
♠ Q 9 7   ♠ J 10 6 4
♥ 6 4 3   ♥ Q J 10
♦ Q J 10 9   ♦ 8 6 5
♣ 8 7 5   ♣ A 4 2
                    ♠ A K 8 2
                    ♥ A K 9 8
                    ♦ A K 7
                    ♣ 10 6

If, in error, you duck the second club, declarer plays three rounds
of hearts and has nine tricks (two spades, three hearts, two
diamonds and two clubs).

If partner had played ♣7 and then ♣5, partner has an even
number (two) of clubs. Declarer has three and you must duck a
second time.

This time you are in the second seat. Declarer leads ♣10, which holds and a second club is played. Should you rise with your ace, or duck a second time? Are clubs like this?

```
              ♣K Q J 9 3
♣A 8 4        [            ]   ♣7 2
              ♣10 6 5
```

Or are they like this?

```
              ♣K Q J 9 3
♣A 8 4        [            ]   ♣7 5 2
              ♣10 6
```

What did partner play on the first club? If ♣7, it is the first layout. You must duck again. If ♣2, play your ace. Don't give declarer an unnecessary club trick.

What about this position?

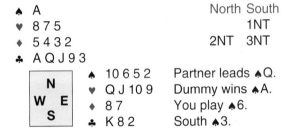

♠	A		North	South
♥	8 7 5			1NT
♦	5 4 3 2		2NT	3NT
♣	A Q J 9 3			

```
          ♠ 10 6 5 2      Partner leads ♠Q.
  N       ♥ Q J 10 9      Dummy wins ♠A.
W   E     ♦ 8 7           You play ♠6.
  S       ♣ K 8 2         South ♠3.
```

Declarer crosses to hand with the ♦A and plays ♣10. Partner plays the ♣4, small from dummy and you play...? You must play ♣2. Partner shows three clubs with ♣4 so declarer has just two clubs. The spade lead knocked out dummy's outside entry, so if declarer is going to get to dummy's club winners it will have to be with a club. If you duck smoothly (easier said than done!) declarer will surely repeat the finesse. Now you win your ♣K and return a spade to knock out declarer's king.

```
              ♣A Q J 9 3
♣7 5 4 2      [            ]   ♣K 8
              ♣10 6
```

With a doubleton king when partner has four cards, you must still duck the king on the first round to cut declarer off from dummy's winners. You hope partner has four clubs when he plays ♣5.

Here is another position when you should think of ducking.

```
              ♣K Q 10 9
♣J 4 3        [          ]   ♣A 8 7 2
              ♣6 5
```

Declarer leads ♣5 towards dummy. Partner plays ♣3, ♣K from dummy and you play...?

You play ♣7, of course. Unless grabbing the trick will allow enough winners to be cashed to beat the contract, you should duck. If you win the first club, declarer might just finesse ♣10 next time and make three tricks. Ducking holds declarer to one trick unless he has outside entries.

Change the position slightly.

```
              ♣K Q 10 9
♣J 4          [          ]   ♣A 8 7 2
              ♣6 5 3
```

And partner should play ♣J on the first round of the suit to warn you that he holds a doubleton.

How many times would you duck this suit?

```
              ♣K J 10 9
♣8 7 5 4      [          ]   ♣A 3 2
              ♣Q 6
```

Declarer leads ♣Q. Partner plays ♣7 and you play ♣2. ♣6 is led, partner plays the ♣4 and dummy the ♣9. Partner's high-low signal shows two or four. If partner has two, declarer has four and can always get to dummy in clubs. If partner has four, win the second trick as declarer is now out of clubs. Either way you should play ♣A on the second round.

Finally, a situation, which is difficult to spot, where it is best not to signal. WE could help declarer make a winning play. If both West and East play high-low, declarer might finesse ♣10 rather than play for the suit to be 3-3. It's easy to signal before you realise what is happening, so watch out for this sort of holding.

```
              ♣K Q 10 3
♣J 9 8 4      [          ]   ♣7 2
              ♣A 6 5
```

Ducking declarer's suit with two stoppers

Declarer will sometimes duck the opening lead, when he has two stoppers in the suit led. Defenders can do the same.

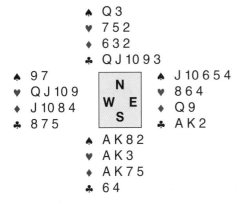

```
                ♠ Q 3
                ♥ 7 5 2
                ♦ 6 3 2
                ♣ Q J 10 9 3
 ♠ 9 7                        ♠ J 10 6 5 4
 ♥ Q J 10 9       N           ♥ 8 6 4
 ♦ J 10 8 4    W     E        ♦ Q 9
 ♣ 8 7 5          S           ♣ A K 2
                ♠ A K 8 2
                ♥ A K 3
                ♦ A K 7 5
                ♣ 6 4
```

South's 2NT opening is raised to 3NT and partner leads the ♥Q. Declarer ducks the first heart and wins the second round.

At trick three, declarer plays ♣4 and partner follows with ♣5, showing three clubs. It may look safe to win ♣K, but see what happens. If you win and play another heart, declarer wins and leads clubs until you take your ace. ♠Q is the entry to dummy to cash the clubs.

Go back to that first club trick. Suppose you duck ♣9. If declarer plays another club you can win and clear the hearts. But as declarer started with a doubleton club, he has not got another club to lead to establish the suit. If he crosses to ♠Q, he can set up the club winners but now has no entry to cash them.

How can you know to duck with two stops? Partner's ♣5 was the lowest missing club, so partner has three clubs. If partner has three, declarer has two.

If you had held ♣A Q x and dummy the ♣K J 10 9 3, it would still be right (but a bit harder) to duck the first club.

Defenders should consider ducking in the suit declarer tries to set up. It rarely costs a trick.

Knocking out dummy's entry

This is a more advanced topic; you can omit this page if you want!

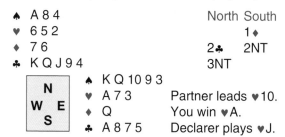

	North	South
		1♦
	2♣	2NT
	3NT	

♠ K Q 10 9 3
♥ A 7 3
♦ Q
♣ A 8 7 5

Partner leads ♥10.
You win ♥A.
Declarer plays ♥J.

Count the points – you have 15, dummy has 10. To rebid 2NT shows 15-16, so that leaves no points for partner. Don't hope partner holds ♥K 10 9 8 7 and declarer ♥Q J, so that we can cash five heart tricks straight away. Remember partner hasn't got any points! Declarer has ♥K Q J for sure. So WE cannot cash lots of heart tricks.

To make 3NT declarer will need to bring in dummy's clubs but you can hold up ♣A until declarer is out of clubs. If you knock out ♠A now, declarer won't have an entry to get back to dummy to cash the club winners.

Lead ♠K. If declarer ducks ♠A, lead ♠Q. Make sure that entry goes. You may give away one spade trick but you stop three club tricks. Your partner will congratulate you for your good defence!

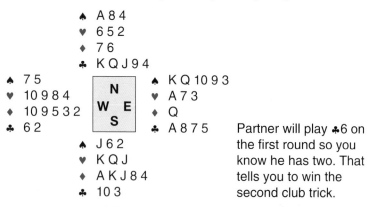

♠ A 8 4
♥ 6 5 2
♦ 7 6
♣ K Q J 9 4

♠ 7 5
♥ 10 9 8 4
♦ 10 9 5 3 2
♣ 6 2

♠ K Q 10 9 3
♥ A 7 3
♦ Q
♣ A 8 7 5

♠ J 6 2
♥ K Q J
♦ A K J 8 4
♣ 10 3

Partner will play ♣6 on the first round so you know he has two. That tells you to win the second club trick.

3NT might still make, but it is likely to go down.

The Merrimac Coup

This is a more advanced topic; you can omit this page if you want!

The last deal showed that switching to your spade sequence could knock out dummy's entry. The Merrimac Coup features a switch to an unsupported honour to knock out dummy's entry

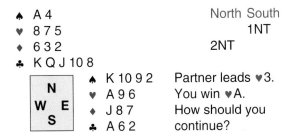

♠ A 4
♥ 8 7 5
♦ 6 3 2
♣ K Q J 10 8

N
W   E
S

♠ K 10 9 2
♥ A 9 6
♦ J 8 7
♣ A 6 2

North South
　　　　1NT
2NT

Partner leads ♥3.
You win ♥A.
How should you
continue?

Declarer will surely need those clubs for 2NT. Holding up your ♣A won't be good enough because ♠A is an entry to cash the clubs. You must drive out ♠A before the clubs are set up. But how? The answer is obvious, once you think of it. Lead a spade. It is not enough to lead a small spade; declarer may be able to win in hand. You must lead ♠K!

If ♠A is taken, the entry has gone. If declarer ducks ♠K, you can lead another spade to force out ♠A. When you win ♣A, you play ♥9 to set up our heart winners. The lead of ♠K gave a trick but two spades, one heart, two diamonds and two clubs were not enough for 2NT as the deal was:

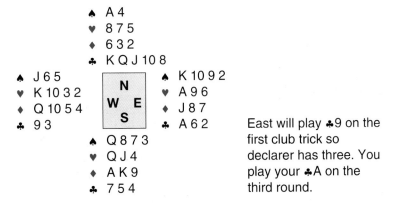

　　　　♠ A 4
　　　　♥ 8 7 5
　　　　♦ 6 3 2
　　　　♣ K Q J 10 8

♠ J 6 5
♥ K 10 3 2
♦ Q 10 5 4
♣ 9 3

N
W   E
S

♠ K 10 9 2
♥ A 9 6
♦ J 8 7
♣ A 6 2

　　　　♠ Q 8 7 3
　　　　♥ Q J 4
　　　　♦ A K 9
　　　　♣ 7 5 4

East will play ♣9 on the first club trick so declarer has three. You play your ♣A on the third round.

Summary

- WE give count signals on declarer's lead. A high then a lower card is an even number. A low then higher one shows an odd number.

- Count signals are particularly useful when there is a long suit in dummy with no outside entry and WE have the ace of the suit.

- WE don't have to win a trick because WE can. It may be better to duck to stop the long suit being established.

- When dummy is short of entries and has a long suit to be set up, try to remove dummy's entry before the winners are established.

Quiz on count signals

♠ 4 3
♥ 8 5 4
♦ K Q J 10 6
♣ 5 3 2

North	South
	2NT
3NT	

	N	
W		E
	S	

♠ A 10 9
♥ K 9 6
♦ A 8 7
♣ Q 10 6 4

Partner leads ♥3 to ♥4, ♥K and ♥A. Declarer leads ♦2, partner plays ♦3. What do you play to tricks two, three and four?

Partner either has one diamond, in which case declarer has four; or three diamonds, when declarer has two. Play ♦7 to trick two, ♦A to trick three and ♥9 to trick four. Declarer cannot get to dummy.

```
                    ♣K Q 6
        ♣8 4      ┌───────────┐  ♣J 7 3 2
                  └───────────┘
                    ♣A 10 9 5
```

Declarer plays a small club to dummy's ♣Q, cashes ♣K and then leads ♣6. How should WE (West and East) follow suit?

The system says West should play ♣8, then ♣4. East should play ♣7, then ♣2. But when East follows to the third club, South might guess the 4-2 distribution and finesse ♣10. On this hand, it is much better if WE both follow upwards and ignore count signals. This position is easier to spot on paper than at the table!

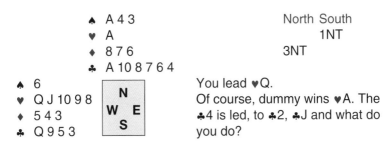

♠ A 4 3
♥ A
♦ 8 7 6
♣ A 10 8 7 6 4

♠ 6
♥ Q J 10 9 8
♦ 5 4 3
♣ Q 9 5 3

North South
        1NT
3NT

You lead ♥Q.
Of course, dummy wins ♥A. The ♣4 is led, to ♣2, ♣J and what do you do?

You can see ten clubs. Partner has followed suit, so declarer has precisely ♣K J. If you win ♣Q declarer has five club tricks. Declarer has ♠A to get to dummy after cashing ♣K. If you duck you may never make a club trick, but declarer only makes three clubs and that puts him one down.

Play ♣3. Declarer had ♠K 8 7 5 ♥K 7 4 2 ♦K 9 2 ♣K J.

♠ K Q 9
♥ 5 3 2
♦ 8 7
♣ K Q J 10 9

♠ 8 6
♥ A K J 10 9
♦ K 5 4 3
♣ 7 5

North South
        1NT
2NT

You lead ♥K.
Dummy plays ♥2. Partner plays ♥4. Declarer plays ♥6.
What should you do at trick two?

Partner's ♥4 is showing either one or three hearts. The lead of the king demands the unblock of any honour held, so partner doesn't have ♥Q. With no honour, partner gives a count signal. If partner has three hearts declarer only has two and ♥Q will drop when your ace is played. Lead ♥A with confidence that you are about to take the first five tricks.

If partner shows out on ♥A, lead ♥9 (suit preference for diamonds) to set up your heart winners.

8 discarding

Often declarer cashes tricks in a long suit when he gains the lead. When your cards in that suit run out, you have to discard. Declarer might cash the suit hoping that you will discard badly.

What your discard means

Apart from showing you have no cards left in the suit on which you discard, the card you throw is used to show where you have values. A small card discourages the suit thrown and a big card shows interest.

Play HELD when you discard
High card is **E**ncouraging
Low card is **D**iscouraging.

The general rule when discarding is to keep winners and throw losers. Unfortunately you cannot always tell which cards might become winners in the future. Here are some general principles, which often work.

When discarding, keep length with dummy

Suppose you can see four spades in dummy and you have four spades too. Your spades may not look like winners but often they stop dummy's fourth card becoming a winner. Look at this layout.

```
                    ♠A Q 8 5
    ♠J 6 2      [              ]    ♠9 7 4 3
                    ♠K 10
```

Hang on to all four spades or dummy's ♠8 will become a winner.

Keep length with declarer and dummy's long suits.

You can't see declarer's hand, so you must remember the suits declarer showed in the bidding when deciding your discard. The auction went:

South	North
1NT	2♣
2♠	3NT

Suppose dummy went down with four hearts and, after winning trick one, declarer cashed them. This time the spades are:

```
              ♠K 9
 ♠7 6 2    [==========]  ♠J 10 4 3
              ♠A Q 8 5
```

You can't see declarer's spades but they are there. Hang on to all four spades, until declarer throws one. If South had bid 2♦ over 2♣, you could safely throw a spade, but should keep the minors.

When discarding, protect your high cards

Suppose you hold ♠Q 8 5. Maybe you can work out who has the ♠A and ♠K. Maybe you can see them in dummy. Either way, you need those two little spades so that when the ace and king are cashed your queen will not fall beneath one of them.

You should keep two small cards to protect an honour whether it is the ace, king, queen or jack. Look at this suit. If declarer cashes dummy's last winner in another suit and spades are:

```
              ♠Q 8 5 2
 ♠J 10 2   [==========]  ♠A 4 3
              ♠K 9 6
```

If you throw a spade from ♠A 4 3, declarer can play a small spade from dummy towards his king and duck on the second round. Look and see that WE had two spade tricks until you threw that spade.

```
              ♠Q 8 5 2
 ♠10 6 2   [==========]  ♠K 4 3
              ♠A J 9
```

The king needs protection too. Here both East and West have vital cards. If East throws a small spade, declarer can finesse ♠J and play ♠A, dropping ♠K. If West throws a spade, declarer can lead ♠Q, you must cover with ♠K, but West's ♠10 drops under ♠J and ♠9 is a winner.

Discarding when you have no easy choice

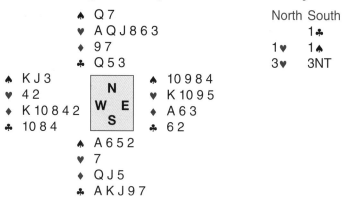

	North	South
♠ Q 7		1♣
♥ A Q J 8 6 3	1♥	1♠
♦ 9 7	3♥	3NT
♣ Q 5 3		

West leads ♦4. East wins ♦A and returns ♦6. West must duck the second diamond, leaving East with a diamond to play as an entry to the winners. If West doesn't duck, declarer can easily set up a heart trick and make his contract.

South plays five rounds of clubs. West follows to three clubs and should first discard the ♠J, a high card to show a high spade (HELD see page 54). West's second discard should be ♥2, a useless card.

East wants to keep four spades, as spades are declarer's second suit, four hearts, keeping length with dummy's suit and a diamond to maintain communication with partner. East has to make three discards on the clubs. Two hearts can be spared but the last discard is awkward.

East must hang onto that ♦3 at all costs. That means a spade must go, trusting that partner's ♠J means he can cover that suit. The heart finesse is the best shot for the ninth trick, but any play by declarer leads to defeat.

> When discarding, keep a card in partner's suit.

Unless it is impossible that you will gain the lead, you must retain at least one card in partner's suit so you can put him in to cash his winners.

Keep your long suit winners

There is no point setting up winners in your long suit, if you then throw them away. You may need to keep your entry too.

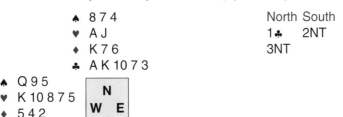

♠ 8 7 4
♥ A J
♦ K 7 6
♣ A K 10 7 3

♠ Q 9 5
♥ K 10 8 7 5
♦ 5 4 2
♣ 6 4

North	South
1♣	2NT
3NT	

As West, you lead ♥7, your fourth highest. Dummy plays ♥J. Partner plays ♥3. Declarer overtakes with ♥Q to lead ♣J for a finesse but East wins ♣Q and returns ♥9, setting up three winners for West.

West has to make three discards on clubs and must keep the hearts. East will get in and he has a third heart to put West in. South hasn't got four hearts as he did not respond 1♥ to 1♣. It looks like West should throw three diamonds and keep three spades, to protect ♠Q.

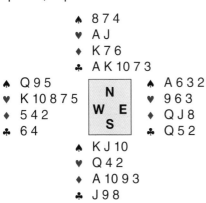

♠ 8 7 4
♥ A J
♦ K 7 6
♣ A K 10 7 3

♠ Q 9 5
♥ K 10 8 7 5
♦ 5 4 2
♣ 6 4

♠ A 6 3 2
♥ 9 6 3
♦ Q J 8
♣ Q 5 2

♠ K J 10
♥ Q 4 2
♦ A 10 9 3
♣ J 9 8

East makes two discards. He must keep three diamonds, his small heart and ♠A. He should throw ♠6 then ♠2, HELD to show good spades. After the clubs, South plays ♠4 from dummy. East must rise with ♠A and play his heart so that West can cash his three hearts for one down.

Signal for the lead you want

♠ 3 2	You are East, defending a no trump
♥ A K 10 9 8	contract. Partner leads a spade, won by
♦ 5 4 3	declarer, who cashes four diamond
♣ 8 7 6	tricks. Your problem is what to throw on
	the fourth diamond to send a signal.

The ♥10 is a very big heart saying 'I like hearts. This is where I have a useful card and I would really like a heart lead.'

On that hand you could afford to throw ♥10, as you would still have ♥A K 9 8, but often you cannot afford to throw a big card in the suit you want without giving declarer a trick. If you hold this hand you cannot afford a high heart.

♠ 3 2	Throw ♣2. This low card shows you
♥ A K 10 9	have no interest in clubs. The inference
♦ 5 4 3	is that your values are in one of the
♣ 8 7 6 2	other suits

Watch the small cards

	♠ A K Q	North South
	♥ Q 9 8	1NT
	♦ K 10 7 6	3NT
	♣ J 7 3	

♠ 10 9 5
♥ 7 5 2
♦ A 9 4 3
♣ 10 6 4

```
    N
  W   E
    S
```

As West, you lead ♦3 against 3NT. It's the fourth highest of your only 4-card suit but it proves to be a poor lead when partner produces ♦5 and declarer wins ♦J. Declarer plays back ♦Q at trick two, you win your ♦A and your partner throws ♣2.

You have not found the killing lead. WE can take no more diamonds, whilst declarer has three diamond tricks. What now?

It will give nothing away to play back a diamond and if you had all the missing high cards it could well be right to do so. Sometimes a passive defence works well. Here a switch might set up winners for our side in another suit. Which suit?

Trust partner. That ♣2 discard says 'Don't play clubs.' Looking at dummy, partner can hardly want a spade. So play a heart and look smug when partner produces ♥A K J 6 and cashes four heart tricks to get 3NT one down.

What if partner had thrown ♥2 on the second diamond instead of a club? That really does look like a signal for clubs. Try playing ♣10 as you are leading through dummy's ♣J. This time find partner with ♣K Q 9 5 and ♥A as an entry, just enough to beat 3NT.

If partner throws a spade it shows no clear-cut interest in either suit. Partner may well have one honour in each of the other suits. In that case exit with a diamond and leave declarer to do all the work.

Watch the number of pips on the cards partner discards.

Summary

- Your first discard in a suit shows your attitude to the suit you discard. Play HELD, high encourages, low discourages.

- A high card followed by a small card is a signal that positively says 'Lead this suit. I hold it.' It tells partner it is safe to discard that suit.

- Use the highest card you can spare for an encouraging signal.

- Throw losers and keep all your winners – if you can.

- Keep length with dummy's long suit and any suit bid by declarer.

- Keep two small cards to protect any honours you hold.

- Unless completely without an entry, keep a card in partner's suit.

- If you discard the suit partner led, throw the card you would have led back, see page 26. This gives partner a count in the suit.

- Watch partner's discards and note which suit partner is keeping.

- The card partner uses to establish his long suit is often a suit preference card, see page 35. This is like giving a high-low signal.

Practise your signals and discards

♠	K Q 4		North South
♥	Q 9 6		1NT
♦	K 10 7		3NT
♣	K J 5 3		

♠ 10 9 5
♥ 8 7
♦ 5 4 3
♣ A 9 7 6 4

```
    N
  W   E
    S
```

As West, you lead ♣6.
Partner shows out, playing
♠3. Declarer wins ♣Q and
plays ♣2. How do you defend?

Win ♣A. Partner throws ♦6. Don't duck the club or declarer may have nine tricks. Partner has thrown small spades and diamonds to show good hearts. So switch to a heart. Partner has ♥A K J 3 2 for two down.

♠	K Q 4		North South
♥	8 7 6		1NT
♦	K 10 7		3NT
♣	K Q J 10		

♠ A 9 5
♥ K Q J 10 9
♦ 5 4 3
♣ 6 4

```
    N
  W   E
    S
```

As West, you lead ♥K. It wins.
You play ♥Q. Partner discards
♣2. Declarer wins ♥A, cashes
four clubs. What do you discard?

First throw ♠9 then ♠5. Show your entry and tell partner he can discard spades but should keep diamonds.

♠	Q 5 3		North South
♥	9 7 5		2NT
♦	9 3		3NT
♣	K Q 9 8 5		

```
    N
  W   E
    S
```

♠ 10 8 7 4 2
♥ A Q 3 2
♦ 10 8
♣ 4 2

You are East. Partner leads ♦4
to ♦3, ♦8 and ♦A. Three
rounds of clubs are played.
Partner wins ♣A on third round.
What do you discard?

Declarer has 20-22 points, dummy has seven, and you have six. There is just room for partner to have the ♥K, so play ♠2.

♠ J 5 3
♥ 8 7 5
♦ 9 3
♣ K Q 9 8 5

	N	
W		E
	S	

♠ 4 2
♥ K Q J 10 9
♦ 5 2
♣ J 10 4 2

Partner leads ♠A. You play ♠2.
Partner continues ♠K, ♠Q and
♠10. Declarer started with four
small spades. What two discards
do you make?

You can't spare a club or declarer has five club tricks. Throw ♥K.
When discarding from a solid sequence, throw the card you would
have led. Next throw ♦2. Only three heart tricks are needed to
beat 1NT.

Quiz on reading partner's signal

The bidding is 1NT raised to 3NT for all these questions.

1) You lead ♦Q, top of a broken sequence ♦Q J 9 8 2. The trick
   is won with dummy's ♦A. Partner follows suit. What kind of
   signal will partner make? Look back to page 22 for help with
   the answer.

2) You lead your fourth highest heart from ♥Q 10 8 4. Dummy
   has ♥A K and wins trick one. What does partner card tell you?
   Look back to page 22 for help with the answer.

3) Declarer now cashes four club tricks. Partner only has two
   clubs. What do the cards partner plays to those four tricks tell
   you? Look back to pages 45 and 54 for help with the answer.

4) Your partner leads what is clearly a long suit. First the king,
   then the queen. Declarer started with Axx and holds up his
   ace until the third round. Partner has several cards that he
   could lead to trick three. What can you tell from the card he
   chooses to lead? Look back to pages 34–35 for help with the
   answer.

On 1 and 2, partner shows attitude to the lead, high if holding
helpful cards. On 3, clubs high-low to give count, then attitude to
suits discarded. On 4, card led shows in which suit his entry lies.

Look at the pages indicated for more detail about these answers.

9 beating the contract

Having reached the halfway point in this book and the end of the section on defending against no trump contracts, let's put it all together to beat all the opponents' contracts.

If you knew exactly what cards everybody held, you would know what contracts to bid, you would know just how to play or defend a hand – but bridge would be a boring game, not worth playing. When defending you build a picture of the unseen hands without being shown the cards so you can work out what to do.

You may have wondered why computers, so successful at playing chess, cannot do the same at bridge. One big problem in bridge is the difficulty of linking together the two halves of the game. How can the lessons from the bidding be taken forward into the defence?

The information from the bidding

Think not just what opponents bid, but what they didn't bid.

- North opens 1♦ and South replies 1NT, South won't have a 4-card major. South's longest suit is probably clubs. Think before you lead a club.

- When South's opening 1NT is raised directly to 3NT they may be short in the majors because they didn't look for a major suit fit. Prefer a major suit to a minor.

- When South's 1NT is raised to 2NT and South bids 3NT, it is likely the contract is short on high cards. With a good hand, consider a passive lead, which does not give tricks away.

- Could partner have overcalled? Failure to do so is a positive action that may mean partner has no 5-card suit or only a very weak one.

Remember, not everybody plays the same system as you, so be clear what opponents' bids mean. Opponents can make mistakes in the bidding, so try not to trust everything they say and do!

Working out what to lead

The opening lead is your chance to get the defence off to a good start. Take your time. Evaluate all the clues from the bidding. First choose the suit and then the right card in that suit.

Reading the lead

The card you lead is a signal to partner about what you hold in that suit. The partnership agreements about which card to lead from a given holding are there to help you and partner defend well. Keep to them!

In third seat, playing after dummy, it is possible to deduce quite a lot. Suppose partner leads the ♦6 and this is what you can see.

	♦7 5 3	
♦6 led	[ ]	♦9 8 4
	?	

Assuming the lead of ♦6 is fourth highest, because that is our agreement, you use Rule of Eleven, 11 − 6 = 5. You can see three of the cards higher than the ♦6, so declarer has two.

Could declarer have the ♦A K? No, that gives partner ♦Q J 10 6 or ♦Q J 10 6 2 and the agreed lead would have been ♦Q.

Could declarer have ♦K Q? Unlikely, it would mean partner had led fourth highest from ♦A J 10 6 rather than the normal ♦J, top of an internal sequence. Similarly, with ♦K J 10 6 2, ♦J would be led.

Could declarer have ♦K J or ♦K J 2? Yes, that would give partner ♦A Q 10 6 2 or ♦A Q 10 6, where ♦6 would always be led.

The opening leader can draw deductions too. Remember this problem? What is South's precise spade holding?

	♠6 2	
♠J 8 5 4 3	[ ]	♠10 played
	♠K played	

As you hold ♠J, partner cannot have ♠A, ♠K or ♠Q since third player plays high. Partner cannot have the ♠9 as with ♠10 9 he would play ♠9. So declarer has precisely ♠A K Q 9, but not five spades if he opened 1NT. Partner has ♠10 7.

Placing the high cards

What should you think about when the lead is made and dummy goes down? Whether you are first or third player, ask yourself questions like:

■ Does dummy have the shape you expected? If not, have you misunderstood the bidding? You can ask your opponents to explain what their bids mean when it is your turn to play.

■ If dummy appears too weak to raise 1NT to 3NT, check the strength of the 1NT bid. Some people play 14–16 or 16–18 instead of 12–14.

■ Count dummy's points. Add those to the ones you hold and the values you think declarer has shown. Deduct from 40. That tells you how many points partner is likely to have.

■ Does the lead help place the points in the suit led? If the 1NT opener has ♠A K Q, he only has 3-5 points in the other suits.

Placing the high cards will stop you embarking on a defence, which needs partner to have a hand he could not possibly hold.

♠ K 9 8 7	
♥ K Q J 3	
♦ A Q 9 8	
♣ J	

West	North	East	South
1♣	dble	pass	1NT
pass	3NT	all pass	

♠ Q J 10 5
♥ A 2
♦ 3
♣ A K 9 8 5 4

```
    N
  W   E
    S
```

You lead ♣A.
Dummy plays ♣J.
Partner plays ♣2.
Declarer plays ♣3.

Count points. 14 from you, 16 in dummy, about 8 from South. Partner has only a couple of points at most. It looks attractive to switch to ♠Q, but it is pointless. Partner cannot have the ♠A. Better to hope partner has ♣10 and declarer has ♣Q 7 6 3. Play ♣K, drop partner's ♣10 and knock out declarer's ♣Q. Declarer will not have enough tricks before having to lose to ♥A.

Declarer had ♠A 6 4 ♥10 5 4 ♦K 7 4 ♣Q 7 6 3.

Working out the distribution

Working out the distribution of the suits is harder, but remember one thing – everybody has precisely 13 cards. Any more or any less and you are not playing bridge! Think about this auction.

South	North
1♥	1♠
2♦	2♥
2NT	3NT

What can you say about the opponents' hands? Where will the high cards be? Start with the points, South has at least 16 for a 2NT game try: with fewer he would pass 2♥. North has at least eight to bid 3NT, but no more than ten, since he only bid 2♥ over 2♦.

Now let's think about the distribution. How many cards in each suit have North and South got?

South has five hearts (bidding two suits shows five cards in the first suit) and at least four diamonds. He has not got four clubs (because he rebid 2♦ not 2♣) but he must have at least two clubs for his 2NT bid, so he cannot have more than two spades and may well have only one.

♠ K Q 6 4 3	North might have a hand like this.
♥ K 5	Useful looking cards and nine points.
♦ J 3 2	Probably only two hearts as he did not
♣ 9 8 3	bid 3♥ over 2♦ or 4♥ over 2NT.

♠ 9	This hand is possible for South, who
♥ A Q 9 8 3	has not promised to be balanced. He
♦ K Q 10 9 5	has a sound club stop and the
♣ A Q	diamonds are a source of tricks. Also
	possible is a diamond fewer and a club
	more.

Knowing all that, what do you lead from this hand?

♠ 10 2	Normally you would lead the unbid suit.
♥ J 10 7 6	But partner should hold the spades.
♦ A 6 4	Lead ♠10. Partner wins and returns a
♣ K J 7 5	club for one down.

What can you deduce about partner's hand on this deal?

♠ 7 4
♥ 8 5 4
♦ K 10 9 5
♣ J 4 3 2

North South
2NT
3NT

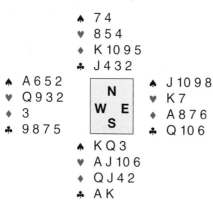

♠ J 10 9 8
♥ K 7
♦ A 8 7 6   Partner leads ♥2 to
♣ Q 10 6   ♥4, ♥K and ♥A

Declarer leads ♦Q, partner plays ♦3. You play ♦8. Declarer leads ♦2. Partner throws ♠6. What now? Declarer has 20–22 points, dummy four and you ten, so partner has at most six points.

Partner's ♥2 shows four, so declarer has four hearts too. Partner's hearts are not ♥Q J 10 2 (lead ♥Q) or ♥J 10 9 2 (lead ♥J) or ♥Q J 9 2. At best partner has ♥Q 10 6 2. If you play ♥7, WE can cash two heart tricks but not three.

Partner has one diamond so must have eight cards in clubs and spades. But he chose a heart lead, so he probably does not have longer spades – a 4414 shape.

Partner has kept four clubs. He has thrown ♠6, which could be second highest from ♠A 6 5 2. So the best guess is partner has a 4414 shape, which makes declarer a 3442 shape.

If a heart is returned partner could easily give declarer a ninth trick in hearts. Win ♦A; do not return hearts but switch to ♠J.

♠ 7 4
♥ 8 5 4
♦ K 10 9 5
♣ J 4 3 2

♠ A 6 5 2
♥ Q 9 3 2
♦ 3
♣ 9 8 7 5

♠ J 10 9 8
♥ K 7
♦ A 8 7 6
♣ Q 10 6

♠ K Q 3
♥ A J 10 6
♦ Q J 4 2
♣ A K

Summary

- Defending a contract is easier if you can build up a picture of the two unseen hands, partner's and declarer's.

- In the bidding, each player tries to describe his hand so that the final contract can be decided. Opponents can listen to that conversation and draw conclusions too, both about shape and high-card strength.

- Information from the bidding includes the bids that were not made as well as those that were.

- Having agreements on which cards to lead, follow suit or discard helps your partner deduce the cards you hold.

- When you see dummy check whether it is what you expected.

- Then count dummy's points and work out the minimum and maximum point count partner can have.

Remember when defending no trumps:

- Think what the bidding, the lead and seeing the dummy tells you.

  Who has the high-card strength?

  What shape are the two unseen hands?

  How are the important suits divided?

- Make a plan for the defence. Your plan must include how to help partner do the right thing. Make sure you don't play cards that will make partner go wrong.

- Check your plan and then get on with it! Don't spend forever thinking and leave no time for playing!

- If something unexpected happens, have a quick rethink. Does it affect your plan?

- The clues as to what you should do are very often there for you to see, if only you remember to look for them.

Practise working out the distribution

What do the auctions given say about the opponents' hands?

North	South	How many spades have North and South?
1♠	2NT	North has five spades and at least four clubs.
3♣	3NT	He passed 3NT so won't have six spades.
pass		South only has two spades or would have bid 3♠ not 3NT.

North	South	What can you say about the distribution?
1♣	1♥	North has 6+ clubs and 16+ points. He hasn't
3♣	3♦	four spades or three hearts, but has a spade
3NT	pass	stop. South probably has five hearts and four (might only have three) diamonds, with no spade stop.

North	South	What is North's distribution?
1♣	1♥	North has longer clubs than spades, but has
1♠	2NT	repeated the spades, say five spades and six
3♠	3NT	clubs. South has 10–12 points, only two
pass		spades but might have three clubs. South can stop hearts and diamonds; his likely shape is 2533 or 2542.

North	South	How many spades has North?
1♠	1NT	North hasn't got a second suit so expect six
2♠	pass	spades. With only five he would pass 1NT.

North	South	How are the majors distributed?
1♠	1NT	North has at least 5-5 in the majors and extra
2♥	2♠	points but not enough to go 4♥. South gave
3♥	pass	preference to spades but passed 3♥ so must have two spades and three hearts and not many points. He responded 1NT, showing 6-9 HCP but must be nearer six than nine.

10 leads against suit contracts

Defending against a suit contract

When there is a trump suit declarer has new opportunities to make tricks and deal with losers – and so do the defence.

♠ 765	South North
♥ A Q 7 5 3	1NT 3NT
♦ J 10	You are West
♣ 6 3 2	What would you lead with this hand?

You would surely lead ♥5, the fourth highest of your longest and strongest suit, in the hope of setting up enough heart tricks to defeat the contract before declarer can make nine tricks.

If partner gains the lead, you expect him to return a heart to help further your plan. If declarer holds something like ♥K J x, you may have given away a trick on the lead, but you have set up four winners to cash later. Look at the complete deal. Declarer hasn't got nine tricks without playing on spades. Partner wins ♠A and returns a heart and 3NT is one down.

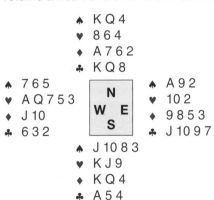

```
            ♠ K Q 4
            ♥ 8 6 4
            ♦ A 7 6 2
            ♣ K Q 8
♠ 7 6 5            ♠ A 9 2
♥ A Q 7 5 3   N    ♥ 10 2
♦ J 10     W   E   ♦ 9 8 5 3
♣ 6 3 2        S   ♣ J 10 9 7
            ♠ J 10 8 3
            ♥ K J 9
            ♦ K Q 4
            ♣ A 5 4
```

Suppose the hands were slightly different and South opened 1♠, raised to 4♠. What would you lead now?

The ♥5 gives away a trick and you won't be able to cash your heart winners later, as declarer can ruff them.

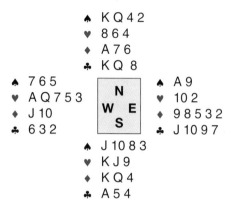

```
            ♠ K Q 4 2
            ♥ 8 6 4
            ♦ A 7 6
            ♣ K Q 8
♠ 7 6 5                    ♠ A 9
♥ A Q 7 5 3      N         ♥ 10 2
♦ J 10        W     E      ♦ 9 8 5 3 2
♣ 6 3 2          S         ♣ J 10 9 7
            ♠ J 10 8 3
            ♥ K J 9
            ♦ K Q 4
            ♣ A 5 4
```

Against 4♠, ♦J is a much safer lead. It gives nothing away. When partner wins ♠A, the best return is ♥10. Declarer covers with ♥J, you win ♥Q, cash your ♥A and lead a little heart for partner to ruff. One down.

If you lead a heart originally, declarer wins ♥J at trick one and now loses just two hearts and ♠A. 4♠ made. Declarer cannot make that vital heart trick without your help.

That ruff to beat 4♠ is the main reason why suit contracts are different. The smallest trump two can beat the biggest ace. In no trumps you can be sure that your ace is a winner, in a suit you can't.

Honour leads

Of course, high cards often will win tricks in a suit contract, which is why WE make leads to set up our high-card tricks. The best leads are solid honour sequences like A K Q, K Q J or Q J 10, which set up winners and rarely cost a trick. Leading the king from K Q J establishes two winners quickly and maybe WE can cash them before they run away.

A good 2-card sequence to lead is AK. For example, with ♥A K 9 7 5 you would lead a low card in no trumps, aiming to set up four heart winners. Against a suit contract you would always lead the ace. Cash your two tricks before they disappear, with the possible bonus that partner can ruff the third round of the suit.

Active or passive?

In the example just discussed WE make different leads against a no trump contract and a suit contract.

Defending against no trumps WE are racing against declarer to set up enough tricks to defeat the contract before declarer can make the number he needs. WE will not achieve this unless WE get busy in our best suit. That is why we often lead a low card from our best suit – ♥5 in the last example. WE lead the fourth highest because that helps partner work out what you hold. This will often give declarer a trick he could not have made otherwise, but it doesn't matter so much because it sets up tricks for later. A lead like this, where WE come out of our corner fighting, is known as an active lead.

In a suit contract, there is no later! Declarer can ruff the suit we have set up. Any trick given away on the lead usually stays away. Often, the main concern when leading against a suit contract is not to give declarer a trick he cannot win without the defence's help. So, in the example above against 4♠, WE make a different lead – ♦J – from the same hand. A lead made with this intention is called a passive lead. WE make declarer work for every trick.

> WE often make an active lead against a no trump contract and a passive lead against a suit contract.

That said, there are no such words as always and never in bridge. Sometimes an active lead against a suit contract is sensible (see Chapter 13) and when declarer looks as if he may have trouble making his contract, a passive lead against no trumps can be a good idea.

Underleading an ace against a suit contract is particularly expensive. In no trumps the lead of ♥4 gives away a trick but sets up two more to cash later. In a suit contract it gives a trick away but gets nothing in return. Even worse, declarer may be able to throw away the second heart in dummy so West may never make his ♥A.

```
                    ♥9 2
    ♥A 8 5 4    [            ]    ♥Q J 10 6
                    ♥K 7 3
```

Partner has bid

As in no trumps, it is normal to lead partner's suit. You should lead the same card against a suit, as you would lead against no trumps, except

Don't underlead an ace against a suit contract.

When not to lead partner's suit

- With length in the suit partner bid, say 5+ cards, it is often pointless to lead the suit since WE only have one trick. Leading the suit is not bad; it just doesn't help the defence.

- Lead a good honour sequence in another suit, KQJ or AK.

- With a singleton and a trump entry, say Ax or Kxx in the trump suit, lead your singleton. When you win your trump trick, lead partner's suit to put partner in to get your ruff.

Partner has not bid

Tend to lead an unbid suit.

♠ 5
♥ Q 10 5 3
♦ Q 9 8 3
♣ 9 7 5 2

	West	North	East	South
	pass	1♥	pass	1♠
	pass	3♠	pass	4♠
	Your lead?			

Not a spade, a singleton trump lead often damages partner's holding. Not a heart, which is North's suit. It won't help the defence to lead it. Clubs or diamonds? Prefer clubs with no honour to diamonds with one.

♠ Q 6 5
♥ Q 10 5 3
♦ Q 9 8 3
♣ Q 2

	West	North	East	South
	pass	1♥	pass	1♠
	pass	3♠	pass	4♠
	Your lead?			

Not a spade, which would only help declarer by finding the ♠Q. Not a heart, it is still North's suit. Not a club, ♣Q from this holding is a very risky lead. That leaves a diamond. Leading from a one-honour suit is dangerous but in this case, leading ♦3 is probably the least of the evils.

Summary

- Think about the bidding before you lead to a trump contract. You will more often, but not always, decide to make a passive lead.

- WE usually lead a suit partner has bid.

- Long suits are less attractive leads, as winners get ruffed.

- Leading a good honour holding sets up cashable winners quickly.

- Make passive leads to avoid giving away tricks that do not come back. A trump may be a good passive lead on some hands.

- Never underlead an ace against a suit contract. Avoid leading a suit headed by an ace unless you have the king as well.

- Usually lead the same card as to no trumps, but lead the top honour from AKxx, KQxx or QJxx, not the fourth highest.

- Lead long suits to give partner a ruff, if you think partner is short in the suit. Lead short suits to get a ruff – see Chapter 12.

Quiz on finding the best lead

♠ A 9 5 2	West	North	East	South
♥ Q J 9		1♦	pass	1♥
♦ 4 2	pass	3♦	pass	3♥
♣ K 10 7 4	pass	4♥	all pass	

Consider each of the four suits in turn. What are the good and bad points for leading that suit? Which card would you lead?

♠	♠A. Leading a suit headed by the ace very often gives away a trick. The ♠A is unlikely to run away.
♥	♥Q. Might stop a ruff, but it is more likely to help than hinder declarer and could give away the trump position.
♦	♦4. North has strong suit, which will provide discards. It can't help your side take tricks.
♣	♣4. Dangerous but WE must set up winners before declarer's club losers are thrown away on dummy's good diamonds.

Quiz on leads against suits

North	South
1♣	1♠
3♠	4♠

You are West. What would you lead from the hands below?

Would your answer change if partner had bid 1♥ over the opening 1♣?

♠ J 6 2
♥ J 7
♦ Q J 7 6
♣ Q J 9 6

♦Q. The diamonds are not quite as strong as the clubs but North bid clubs.
♥J. If partner overcalls lead his suit to cash his winners quickly.

♠ J 6
♥ Q 6 3
♦ J 10 9
♣ J 9 7 5 3

♦J. The 3-card sequence led through the stronger hand may well set up winners.
♥3. If partner overcalls, make the normal heart lead from Q 6 3.

♠ A 6 2
♥ 8 7 5 3 2
♦ 5
♣ 9 7 6 5

Lead the ♦5 whether or not partner bid hearts. You plan to win ♠A then lead a heart. You hope partner can win this trick and lead a diamond for you to ruff.

♠ 5 3 2
♥ K J 6 3
♦ K J 6 3
♣ 9 7

♠2. The red suit holdings make a passive lead attractive and a trump may reduce declarer's ability to ruff. (See Chapter 11.)
♥3. Lead hearts to grab your tricks before declarer can discard his losers on dummy's clubs.

♠ A 6
♥ 8 5 3 2
♦ Q J 10 9
♣ J 10 9

♦Q. The sort of sequence you are pleased to lead. If partner overcalled hearts you may feel you should lead them, but a diamond is more likely to set up winners.

11 when to lead trumps

Some people feel it is not the defender's job to lead trumps. After all, they think, the defence might win a trick by ruffing. In fact, that doesn't happen very often because declarer draws trumps to prevent it. Here are some very good reasons for leading trumps.

Declarer will make his trumps separately

If declarer has shown a 5-card suit, you won't be able to stop those tricks making in his hand. But if dummy has three trumps, every one that is used for a ruff is an extra trick for declarer. We can stop those tricks making by leading trumps. For example, if declarer has shown a two-suiter and dummy has given clear preference to one of the suits, it is quite possible that declarer will be trumping the other suit in dummy.

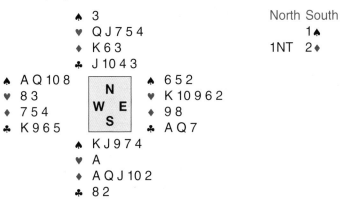

```
                  ♠ 3                     North  South
                  ♥ Q J 7 5 4                      1♠
                  ♦ K 6 3                 1NT    2♦
                  ♣ J 10 4 3
  ♠ A Q 10 8          N           ♠ 6 5 2
  ♥ 8 3          W         E      ♥ K 10 9 6 2
  ♦ 7 5 4            S            ♦ 9 8
  ♣ K 9 6 5                       ♣ A Q 7
                  ♠ K J 9 7 4
                  ♥ A
                  ♦ A Q J 10 2
                  ♣ 8 2
```

North has given preference to diamonds by passing 2♦. In this auction diamonds may only be a 4-card suit, where spades must be at least a 5-card suit, so North must be short in spades. You have good spades; lead a trump to stop them being ruffed.

Declarer wins the trump in dummy then leads a spade. But you win the trick and play another trump, cutting the ruffs available in dummy to just one. Declarer must go down.

When each opponent bids a suit and the final contract is in a third suit, it is likely that ruffs will be available in both hands. A trump lead can sometimes stop declarer making those ruffs.

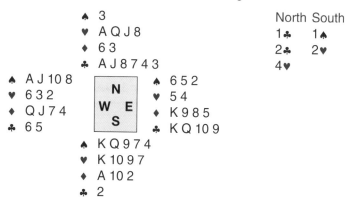

```
              ♠ 3
              ♥ A Q J 8              North  South
              ♦ 6 3                   1♣     1♠
              ♣ A J 8 7 4 3           2♣     2♥
 ♠ A J 10 8        ┌─────┐    ♠ 6 5 2 4♥
 ♥ 6 3 2          N │     │    ♥ 5 4
 ♦ Q J 7 4     W     E    │    ♦ K 9 8 5
 ♣ 6 5            S │     │    ♣ K Q 10 9
                   └─────┘
              ♠ K Q 9 7 4
              ♥ K 10 9 7
              ♦ A 10 2
              ♣ 2
```

♦Q looks a safe enough lead and partner plays ♦9 (encouraging card, see page 24). Declarer wins and plays ♠K. You win, cash a diamond and play a trump, say. Declarer wins and makes a trick in each suit. The six remaining trumps can be made separately by ruffing in each hand. That safe diamond lead makes ten tricks easy for declarer.

Think about the bidding. South has shown at least five spades and four hearts and North has five or six clubs and four hearts. With suits breaking badly, declarer will need to play for ruffs.

Instead of ♦Q, try leading ♥2. Say declarer wins, plays ♣A and ruffs a club, trying to set up his clubs. Then ♠K is led. You win and play a second heart, won in dummy for South to ruff another club. South is now out of trumps and the clubs are not yet set up. Dummy's losing diamond is thrown on ♠Q and a spade ruffed, but it's only nine tricks.

Put out the cards and try all the lines of play you can think of. It only comes to nine tricks when a trump is led. But on ♦Q lead, declarer can manage ten tricks quite easily.

When no other lead is attractive

Sometimes every other lead looks likely to give away a trick.

♠ J 4	The bidding goes 1♠ – 4♠ and you
♥ A Q 6 5	have to find a lead
♦ K J 3	
♣ K J 5 3	

Here a passive lead of your lowest trump ♠4 looks to be best. Leading from any of your tenaces is likely to give a trick away (see page 71).

	North	South
♠ K J 10 6		1♥
♥ 5 4 3		
♦ Q 8 3	1♠	1NT
♣ A 9 8	3♥	4♥

North's 3♥ shows 3-card heart support and South, with a balanced 15–16 shows five hearts by bidding 4♥. You are leading up to a balanced hand with strength, so leading from unsupported honours is likely to cost a trick. A trump lead gives nothing away.

When they are bidding shape not points

	West	North	East	South
♠ 6 5 2	1♥	2♦	3♥	3♠
♥ A K 8 4 3	4♥	4♠	dble	all pass
♦ K Q J	You are vulnerable, opponents are not.			
♣ A 10				

Your non-vulnerable opponents sacrifice against your game. You must not only beat 4♠ but also gain as big a penalty as possible to make up for the lost game. Partner has shown points and the opponents must be bidding on shape, not high cards. They will hope to make tricks using their trumps. Lead a trump and foil their plan. It cannot cost and it may stop some of their ruffs.

Consider a trump lead when your side has lots of points.

Which trump should you lead?

If you have three honours in sequence, KQJ, QJ10 or J109 or two trump honours doubleton, QJ, J10 or 109, lead the top honour. In all other cases, lead your lowest trump. You may be able to use the bigger trump to overruff.

K 6 5   Lead the five if you feel a trump is right.

9 8 2   Lead the two, the nine and eight may be useful.

J 10 4   Lead the four. Partner might have the singleton Q or K.

When not to lead trumps

Having seen that trump leads can be effective, you might try leading trumps more often. Don't be like one player who always leads trumps, except when she has an honour. So with:

```
            ♥A J 9 5
♥?        [            ]   ♥?
            ♥K 10 7 6
```

If West leads a trump declarer's problems are solved. If West doesn't lead a trump, she must have ♥Q. Don't be predictable!

Don't lead a singleton trump

If you have one trump, partner will probably have three or four.

```
            ♥A 9 5 3
♥2        [            ]   ♥Q 10 6
            ♥K J 8 7 4
```

In this position where declarer has nine trumps, declarer is unlikely to take a trump finesse and so will lose a trick to partner's ♥Q. But declarer has no problem if you lead ♥2.

```
            ♥Q 7 5
♥2        [            ]   ♥J 10 4 3
            ♥A K 9 8 6
```

On ♥2 lead, the trick goes, ♥5, ♥10, ♥K. Next, declarer plays to ♥Q, you show out and now declarer can finesse against partner's ♥J.

What would you lead after this auction?

♠	A 6 5 2
♥	3
♦	K Q J 9
♣	A 10 8 3

West	North	East	South
			1♥
dble	all pass		

This is one exception to the rule. When partner passes a takeout double, it shows very good trumps, say ♥K Q J 10 9 8. You must lead a trump, if you can. Either you may stop declarer making his small trumps by ruffing or you may stop a possible ruff in dummy, maybe both.

Don't lead trumps if you have length in trumps.

You would not normally lead trumps from a strong holding of four cards or more. Rather, you should prefer to lead your longest suit and try to make declarer ruff. Making declarer ruff with his long trumps may make him run out of trumps before he has drawn all your trumps. This is called a forcing defence and is discussed fully in Chapter 13.

Summary

- Have a positive reason to lead trumps. Reasons include:
    - ✔ Stopping ruffs in the short trump hand.
    - ✔ Stopping ruffing taking place in both hands (called crossruffing).
    - ✔ Being passive with a strong defending hand.
    - ✔ When the defending side has significantly more high cards.
    - ✔ Partner has passed your takeout double.
    - ✔ Holding honours in all the other suits against a slam.
- Don't lead a singleton trump without a very good reason. It is likely to lose a trump trick by exposing partner's holding.
- Don't lead trumps or a singleton when you have long trumps. Prefer a long suit, forcing declarer to ruff and run out of trumps.
- Lead your lowest trump unless you have a solid sequence.

Practise leading trumps

Without knowing the actual hand you hold, which of these auctions suggests that a trump might be led? Why?

1)
North	South
	1♠
1NT	2♥

2)
North	South
	1♠
2♣	2♥
3♥	4♥

3)
North	South
	2♥
3♥	4NT
5♦	7♥

4)
North	South
	1♠
3♣	3♠
4♠	

5)
North	South
	1♠
2♣	4♠

6)
North	South
	1♥
2♥	2NT
3♥	

7)
West	North	East	South
			1♥
pass	2♥	2♠	pass
pass	3♥		

8)
West	North	East	South
			1♠
dble	all pass		

1) North showed preference for hearts by passing. He would have given preference for spades if he could, since the auction shows at least five spades. With good hearts, North would bid 3♥, so North is very weak or only has three hearts. Consider a trump lead.

2) Both North and South bid another suit first before finding what is likely to be a 4-4 heart fit. There is a strong possibility each is short in the other's first suit. Declarer might go for a crossruff. Consider a trump lead, particularly with strength in the first bid suits.

3) South is strong with very good trumps, since no effort was made to check on partner's heart holding. South hopes North has the right cards that will fill the gaps. Lead a 3-card sequence in a side suit, if held, but otherwise lead a trump from small cards.

4) It is more likely that the opposition have missed a slam than that 4♠ is going down. If the contract is to be beaten we must cash winners quickly. Make an attacking red suit lead, before South's losers disappear on North's clubs.

5) South has a lot of spades but they are not solid. North might have a spade void, so do not even think of a trump lead. It can only help declarer.

6) South has a strong balanced hand with only four hearts, about 17–19 points. With five hearts South would not offer the alternative no trump game. North is weak but does have four or more hearts and probably a shortage somewhere. Consider a trump .

7) First thoughts should be to lead partner's suit. However, North may well be short in spades when he bids on to 3♥, so a trump could turn out well. North might raise to 2♥ with only three hearts but will certainly have four hearts to bid on to 3♥.

8) If you have a trump it should already be on the table. A pass of a takeout double at the one level is always based on very good tricks in the trump suit. You do not want declarer to make a little trump by ruffing either in his hand or in dummy.

Practise opening leads against suits

North	South
	1♠
3♠	4♠

You are West and hold the hands below. What do you lead?

♠ Q 2 ♥ 8 6 ♦ 9 7 5 3 2 ♣ Q J 9 8	Certainly not a trump, A heart could well spoil partner's holding, you have too many diamonds to set up tricks. ♣Q is much more likely to set up winners quickly.
♠ A 7 3 ♥ 9 7 6 4 2 ♦ 8 ♣ Q 7 5 4	This is a good hand to lead a singleton. Even if partner cannot win the first diamond, you can win ♠A and hope to put partner in to get a diamond ruff.
♠ 10 5 ♥ A K 5 3 2 ♦ 9 7 6 4 ♣ 8 6	The ♥A is clearly the best lead. You cash your winners quickly and partner may have a doubleton heart, which can be shown by playing an encouraging high-low signal.
♠ K 8 5 ♥ 4 ♦ A J 7 5 ♣ K Q 9 5 3	You have lots of points so partner can have very few. Do not lead ♥4, you will never get partner in to give you a ruff. Try ♣K to set up a trick there.
♠ K J 10 ♥ 4 ♦ J 7 5 3 ♣ K Q 9 5 3	This time you only have ten points but a singleton is still not a good lead. You don't need ruffs when you have one or two trump tricks. Still lead ♣K.
♠ A J 9 ♥ 10 7 ♦ 10 9 8 5 ♣ Q 9 7 5	With two potential trump tricks, you don't want to try your doubleton heart hoping for a ruff. ♦10 is the safer minor suit lead.
♠ 8 ♥ A Q 6 4 ♦ K J 7 5 2 ♣ 8 5 2	Singleton trump leads often kill partner's trump trick. The red suits are unattractive to lead. This leaves clubs and ♣5, the middle from three is the standard lead.

12 giving and getting ruffs

One of the most satisfying ways of beating a contract is to ruff the opponents' winners. It must be done before trumps are drawn.

Leading a short suit

♠	9 6 5		North	South
♥	3			1♠
♦	J 9 6 5 4		4♠	
♣	J 10 9 2		Your lead?	

When opponents bid to game, they usually have 25 or more points. You have only two points, so partner has some high cards, perhaps as many as 13 points.

Leading your singleton heart stands a good chance of success. You hope partner can win the heart, give you a ruff and get in again to give you a second ruff. With your three trumps, this defence looks good.

♠	A 6 5		North	South
♥	3			1♠
♦	K Q J 9 2		4♠	
♣	K J 10 9		Your lead?	

With the same shape but 14 points you would be wasting your time leading a heart: partner cannot have ♥A or any other entry. Be thankful that you have a solid sequence, lead ♦K.

♠	9 6 5		North	South
♥	A K			1♠
♦	J 9 3 2		4♠	
♣	10 9 8 4		Your lead?	

You would like to get a heart ruff. Lead ♥K then ♥A. This unusual way of leading your honours sends a message to partner 'I have only two hearts'. When on lead, partner will know to lead a heart for you to ruff. Maybe when you see dummy, you will be able to tell where partner's entry is.

Switching to a singleton

```
♠ K 8 6 4                    North  South
♥ J 3                               1♠
♦ K J 10 9                   3♠    4♠
♣ J 7 5
```

```
        N        ♠ 7 5 2
   W         E   ♥ A 9 7 5       You are East.
        S        ♦ 8 7 6 5 4     Partner leads ♥2.
                 ♣ 6             How do you defend?
```

You have four points and dummy has nine, so partner should have some good cards. When you win the ♥A at trick one, you have a choice. Either you play back a heart or you can play back your singleton club. The club seems to offer the best chance. If partner wins the club and gives you a ruff, you can now play the heart to get a second ruff. Two hearts, a club and two ruffs would beat even 3♠.

If you had the singleton ♣A rather than ♣6, you would first cash that ace and then play a heart for partner to give you a club ruff.

A trump signal

On the hand above, you switched to your singleton and got a ruff. You then played a heart, which partner won. He returned a club for you to ruff again. What if partner didn't have ♥K, but he did have ♠A? When he won ♠A, he would need to know if you still held a trump.

The answer is in the order you play your trumps. High-low shows three trumps – exactly the opposite of the count signal in other suits where high-low shows two or four. You began with ♠7 5 2, you ruff the first club with ♠5. On the trump lead you play ♠2, telling partner you have a third trump. With ♠5 2, you would ruff with ♠2 and play ♠5 next.

Playing high then low in the trump suit shows three trumps and a desire to ruff.

This high-low signal is often called a peter. WE peter in declarer's suit in no trumps to show an even number, see page 45. WE peter in declarer's trump suit to show an odd number.

Suit preference signals

You first met the suit preference signal in Chapter 5 in the section on 'showing your entry' (page 34). The idea is to play a high card if you want the higher ranking suit and a low card for the lower ranking suit. WE also use suit preference signals when leading a suit for partner to ruff. Here is an example.

South's 1♠ opening is raised to 3♠ and South goes on to 4♠.

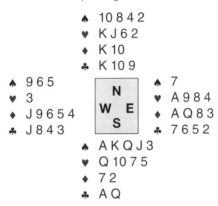

```
              ♠  10 8 4 2
              ♥  K J 6 2
              ♦  K 10
              ♣  K 10 9
♠ 9 6 5           N           ♠ 7
♥ 3                           ♥ A 9 8 4
♦ J 9 6 5 4     W   E         ♦ A Q 8 3
♣ J 8 4 3         S           ♣ 7 6 5 2
              ♠  A K Q J 3
              ♥  Q 10 7 5
              ♦  7 2
              ♣  A Q
```

You lead ♥3. Partner wins ♥A and, hoping you have led a singleton, returns a heart for you to ruff. What do you lead now? The answer lies in the card partner led back. If it was ♥9, a high card, you should play the higher ranking non-trump suit, a diamond. If it was ♥4, a low card, play the lower suit, a club. So the defence should go:

Trick 1   ♥3 led taken by ♥A.
Trick 2   ♥9 returned, ruffed with ♠6.
Trick 3   ♦5 led to ♦K and ♦A.
Trick 4   ♥8 returned, ruffed with ♠5.
Trick 5   ♦4 led to partner's ♦Q.
Trick 6   ♥4 ruffed with the ♠9.

Declarer, with a combined 28 points, is three down before he wins a trick! But look what happens if you return a club at trick three. Declarer makes 4♠ by drawing trumps and discarding one of his losing diamonds on dummy's club winner.

A suit preference signal shows the suit you want led back.

Giving partner a ruff

Sometimes the clue is in the opponents' bidding. Look at this hand and decide what you would lead.

		North	South
♠	9		
♥	A Q 10		1♠
♦	J 9 3 2	2♣	3♣
♣	10 8 6 5 4	3♠	4♠

Did you choose a club lead? The opponents must have eight clubs between their two hands. You have five clubs. Eight plus five makes thirteen, so either the pack has 14 clubs or partner has a void.

It is not enough to select a club lead; you have to say which club. This is your chance to give a suit preference signal. Lead ♣10, a high card asking for the higher non-trump suit.

Partner will ruff and, noticing the card you led, should play a heart to get a second ruff. If declarer has the ♥K, you will have a second heart trick and may be able to give a total of three club ruffs.

Here is a variation on this theme.

		North	South
♠	9		
♥	J 9 3 2		1♠
♦	A Q 10 5	2♣	3♣
♣	A 8 5 4	3♠	4♠

Holding ♣A 8 5 4, you realise partner cannot have more than one club. You lead the ♣A and follow up with the ♣4, a low club this time asking for a diamond not a heart. Clever, isn't it?

		North	South
♠	9 6 5		
♥	A K		1♠
♦	J 9 3 2	4♠	
♣	10 9 8 4	Your lead?	

This hand was on page 83. You led ♥K then ♥A to show a doubleton heart. An alert partner will give you a suit preference signal on the ♥A to tell you which suit to lead to get your ruff.

Signalling to show a doubleton

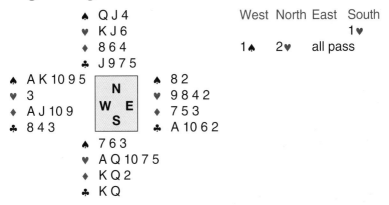

```
              ♠ Q J 4              West  North  East  South
              ♥ K J 6                                  1♥
              ♦ 8 6 4              1♠    2♥     all pass
              ♣ J 9 7 5
♠ A K 10 9 5       N        ♠ 8 2
♥ 3          W         E    ♥ 9 8 4 2
♦ A J 10 9         S        ♦ 7 5 3
♣ 8 4 3                     ♣ A 10 6 2
              ♠ 7 6 3
              ♥ A Q 10 7 5
              ♦ K Q 2
              ♣ K Q
```

Imagine you are East for a moment. Partner leads ♠A. Are you pleased with the lead? Would you like partner to switch to another suit?

Surely partner would not lead ♠A without holding ♠K as well. So if partner continues with spades, you will be able to ruff the third round. How do you let partner know you like the lead? You play a high card to encourage! Remember that on partner's lead we give signals that encourage or discourage a continuation (see page 22 onwards).

So you play ♠8 and when partner continues with ♠K, you play ♠2. Partner leads ♠10 and you ruff with ♥2 (the lowest trump from two or four). Even though no more spade ruffs are available, partner's card is suit preference and you should play a diamond.

Partner beats declarer's ♦K with ♦A and returns ♦J. When you get in with ♣A, you play a diamond to get declarer one down.

On this deal partner could read your high-low signal as a doubleton. Suppose dummy had had three small spades and you had held ♠Q 8 2. You would still play ♠8 to encourage partner to continue spades since you do not want a switch.

Summary

■ Lead a singleton when you have a bad hand and can expect partner to have some high cards. Do not lead a singleton from a good hand. Partner's only defensive trick may be ruined by your singleton lead.

■ If you win the lead in third hand, consider switching to a singleton rather than returning partner's suit immediately.

■ If you have A K alone, lead the king then the ace. Expect a suit preference signal from partner on the ace.

■ When ruffing or following to trumps, play the middle then the lower card with three. Follow upwards with two or four.

■ When giving a ruff, choose the card you lead to indicate the suit you want returned.

■ If you make an opening lead where you expect partner to ruff, choose the card you lead as a suit preference signal.

■ If partner leads an ace or a king and you have a doubleton, play high-low to encourage partner to continue.

Summary of when WE play high-low

■ A high card followed by a lower card is called a peter and is always a signal to partner. A peter can have various meanings and WE know which it is by the context in which it is played.

■ On partner's lead a peter is encouraging, asking partner to continue this suit. This applies whether partner or declarer wins the trick.

■ On declarer's lead a peter is a count signal, showing an even number of cards. Low-high shows an odd number.

■ When out of a suit, we discard a high card to encourage the suit discarded. A low card shows nothing of interest in the suit.

■ High-low in declarer's trump suit shows three trumps.

■ Use your high and low cards as a suit preference signal when leading a card for partner to ruff; also for showing your entry to cash the winners you have set up.

Quiz on getting ruffs

		North	South
♠	J 10 4 3	1♣	1♠
♥	A 6	2♠	4♠
♦	7 6		
♣	A K J 10 3		

♠ A K 5
♥ 9 7 5 3 2
♦ Q 9 5 2
♣ 4

As West, do you lead club, diamond or a heart?

It is not easy to decide which suit to lead. Long hearts with no honour are unlikely to set up tricks. Diamonds may actually cost a trick unless partner has ♦K or ♦A, but might set up winners to cash. As you must get in twice with trumps, you have plenty of time to try for a ruff. If partner has a high diamond it could be the entry to give you a club ruff. On balance, trying for the ruff looks best, so lead your singleton ♣4. Dummy's ♣A wins, partner plays ♣9 and declarer ♣8.

What do you make of partner's ♣9?

Partner can tell your lead is a singleton, so ♣9 should be a signal asking for a heart. Perhaps partner has ♥K. The ♠J is led, you win your ♠K.

What do you lead to trick three?

Play ♥7, (second highest with no honour). Declarer takes ♥A and plays another spade. You win, play ♥3, won by partner's ♥K and get your club ruff.

Leading dummy's suit is dangerous, since dummy's clubs will normally be at least a 5-card suit. Declarer may be able to throw diamond losers on the clubs. But no losers can be thrown until trumps are drawn, so the lead is safer because you have the two top trumps – they are always winners!

♠ Q 9 8 7 2
♥ Q 8 4
♦ A K J
♣ Q 8

Here is declarer's hand. Since his trumps are missing the ace and king, you can tell he must have most of the other high cards for his 4♠ bid.

13 the forcing defence

Even though declarer starts with more trumps than WE do, he can still run out of trumps, particularly when they split badly.

♥7 5 3

♥A 6 4 2   [   ]   ♥8

♥K Q J 10 9

Declarer has eight trumps, the defence only five. Four trumps are needed to draw West's trumps, leaving only one spare.

Suppose West leads a suit in which South is short and has to ruff. South now has only the same number of trumps as West. If West can force South to ruff again when he wins his ♥A, West will then have more trumps than South. So a key defensive point is

---

With long trumps, lead a long side suit.

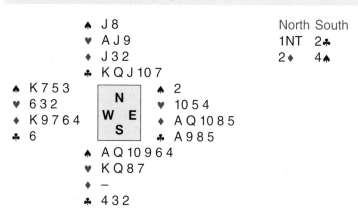

```
              ♠ J 8
              ♥ A J 9                North South
              ♦ J 3 2                1NT    2♣
              ♣ K Q J 10 7           2♦     4♠
  ♠ K 7 5 3               ♠ 2
  ♥ 6 3 2       N         ♥ 10 5 4
  ♦ K 9 7 6 4  W   E      ♦ A Q 10 8 5
  ♣ 6           S         ♣ A 9 8 5
              ♠ A Q 10 9 6 4
              ♥ K Q 8 7
              ♦ —
              ♣ 4 3 2
```

If you lead ♣6, East can win ♣A and give you a ruff, but ♠K is the only other trick you make. Try ♦6 lead. South ruffs, crosses to dummy and plays ♠J. You win ♠K and lead ♦4. South ruffs and is now down to three trumps. If he draws all your trumps, partner can cash diamonds when in with ♣A. If he drives out ♣A first, partner plays a diamond and now declarer has fewer trumps than you.

It is important to make sure you force declarer to ruff in the hand with long trumps. Letting him ruff in the hand with the shorter trump holding just gives him extra tricks.

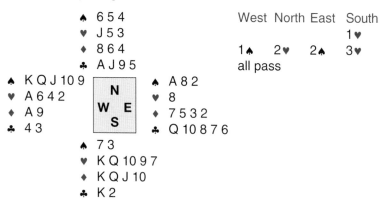

	♠ 6 5 4	West	North	East	South
	♥ J 5 3				1♥
	♦ 8 6 4	1♠	2♥	2♠	3♥
	♣ A J 9 5	all pass			

West hand:
♠ K Q J 10 9
♥ A 6 4 2
♦ A 9
♣ 4 3

East hand:
♠ A 8 2
♥ 8
♦ 7 5 3 2
♣ Q 10 8 7 6

South hand:
♠ 7 3
♥ K Q 10 9 7
♦ K Q J 10
♣ K 2

South has only four losers off the top: two spades, one heart and one diamond. But look what happens when the defence play three rounds of spades. South must ruff this, as he still has two aces to lose.

South plays ♥K. If West wins this trick, to play another spade, the ruff can be taken in dummy, since dummy's spades have been played on the first three tricks. Ruffs in dummy do not shorten declarer's trumps and do the defence no good. So West must not win his ♥A until the third round, when dummy will be out of trumps.

If South plays a third trump, West's fourth spade forces another ruff from South, making ♥6 the only trump left. When West wins ♦A, he can cash the fifth spade for two down.

Declarer might play diamonds when the second trump is ducked, before all dummy's trumps have gone. But West can win ♦A, cash ♥A to draw dummy's last trump, and then play his fourth spade. His entry to cash his fifth spade comes by trumping one of declarer's winners.

However declarer plays the cards, he will run out of trumps. Put out the cards and play the hand. Making declarer ruff is not a waste of time.

Make the long trump hand ruff to shorten his trumps.

The forcing defence can still work if declarer's trumps divide 4-4, even though making one hand ruff leaves four trumps in the other. Look at this deal:

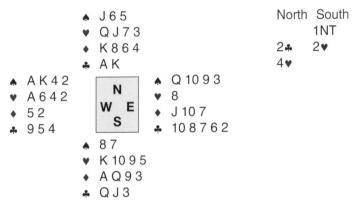

♠ J 6 5	North South
♥ Q J 7 3	1NT
♦ K 8 6 4	2♣ 2♥
♣ A K	4♥

West leads ♠A K. East plays an encouraging ♠10, followed by ♠3 to show ♠Q. West plays another spade, which South ruffs.

If West wins the first or second trump it will be no use playing another spade as South can ruff and then enter dummy with ♣A to complete drawing trumps. West must duck both ♥Q and ♥K, letting them win so that South is out of trumps when West wins his ♥A. West wins the third trump and plays another spade, to force out North's last trump. If South stops playing trumps, West will make ♥6 by ruffing a diamond.

If West wins the first trump and plays his last spade, he is giving what is called a ruff and discard. A loser can be thrown from dummy and the ruff taken with South's last trump. Remember, South is, at this point, the short trump hand. Giving a ruff and discard is rarely good defence. Here it would let the contract make even if South did not have ♦Q, as one of North's losing diamonds could be thrown and the other played on ♣Q.

Avoid giving a ruff and discard.

A ruff and discard allows declarer to decide in which hand he wants to take the ruff and which suit in the other hand he wants to discard – it gives declarer an extra trick he could not win without defender's help.

Summary

- If the long trump hand can be made to ruff the defence's winners, it can sometimes cause declarer to run out of trumps and lose control of the hand.

- It can be good defence to lead a suit that can be ruffed by one, and only one, of the declaring hands. But don't lead a suit when both opponents are void in that suit. Avoid giving a ruff and discard.

- With long trumps, lead a long suit to make declarer ruff.

Quiz on forcing declarer

What lead should West make to 4♥? How can 4♥ be beaten? After two rounds of trumps South will play ♦5 to ♦Q in dummy.

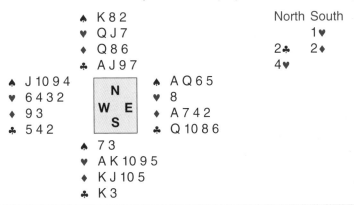

```
          ♠ K 8 2              North  South
          ♥ Q J 7                       1♥
          ♦ Q 8 6              2♣     2♦
          ♣ A J 9 7           4♥

♠ J 10 9 4    ┌──────┐    ♠ A Q 6 5
♥ 6 4 3 2     │  N   │    ♥ 8
♦ 9 3         │W   E │    ♦ A 7 4 2
♣ 5 4 2       │  S   │    ♣ Q 10 8 6
              └──────┘
          ♠ 7 3
          ♥ A K 10 9 5
          ♦ K J 10 5
          ♣ K 3
```

The best lead is ♠J and the defence play three rounds of spades. South ruffs and starts to draw trumps. When East shows out on the second round, South has a problem. If he draws all four of West's trumps, he too will be out of trumps and East can cash a spade when he wins ♦A.

South must stop playing trumps after two rounds and knock out ♦A. If South plays a diamond to ♦Q and East wins ♦A, the contract is safe. East can lead any suit back, South just wins and draws all the trumps. West must play ♦9 on the first diamond to show a doubleton. If East ducks the first diamond and wins the second, he can give West a diamond ruff.

South plays 4♠. Can it be beaten?

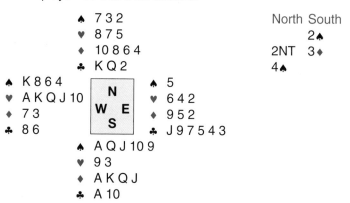

```
              ♠ 7 3 2                    North  South
              ♥ 8 7 5                            2♠
              ♦ 10 8 6 4                  2NT    3♦
              ♣ K Q 2                     4♠
  ♠ K 8 6 4              ♠ 5
  ♥ A K Q J 10    N      ♥ 6 4 2
  ♦ 7 3        W     E   ♦ 9 5 2
  ♣ 8 6           S      ♣ J 9 7 5 4 3
              ♠ A Q J 10 9
              ♥ 9 3
              ♦ A K Q J
              ♣ A 10
```

West leads top hearts. South ruffs the third heart, crosses to ♣K and takes a trump finesse. West must duck! South probably plays ♠A next. If South stops playing trumps, West gets a diamond ruff. If South continues trumps, West gets in with ♠K and forces out the last spade by leading another heart.

If South plays ♠J, not ♠A, after the finesse wins, 4♠ cannot be beaten and South gets 'Well played' from partner. Try it and see.

What do you lead on these hands? Why?

```
  ♠ 6 5 4 3              North  South
  ♥ 2                            1♠
  ♦ A K Q 10             2NT    3♥
  ♣ 9 8 6 4             4♠
```

♦A. The lead you would make even if you didn't have four trumps. Leading a singleton in declarer's second suit is not a good idea.

```
  ♠ A K Q 2              North  South
  ♥ 6 5                          1♠
  ♦ Q J 9 7 5            2♣     3♣
  ♣ 8 4                 3♠     4♠
```

♦Q. Don't be tempted to lead off the top spades and draw two of declarer's trumps for one of yours. Aim to make ♠2 the setting trick by forcing declarer to ruff diamonds and run out of trumps.

14 trump promotion

In the previous chapter we saw that making declarer ruff with his long trumps could help the defence. This chapter is about another way that making declarer ruff can lead to extra tricks for the defenders.

Trumps really are magic cards. Suppose a suit is divided as shown

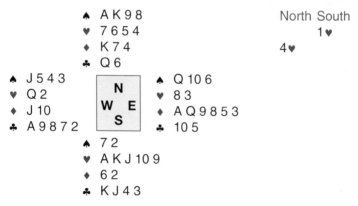

```
                    ♥7 6 5 4
      ♥Q 2          [            ]        ♥8 3
                    ♥A K J 10 9
```

In no trumps declarer plays out the ♥A then the ♥K. When ♥Q drops he has five heart tricks. But this suit may only make four tricks in a suit contract. Here's how the impossible can happen:

```
              ♠ A K 9 8              North  South
              ♥ 7 6 5 4                      1♥
              ♦ K 7 4                  4♥
              ♣ Q 6
   ♠ J 5 4 3          ┌──────┐    ♠ Q 10 6
   ♥ Q 2              │  N   │    ♥ 8 3
   ♦ J 10            W│      │E   ♦ A Q 9 8 5 3
   ♣ A 9 8 7 2        │  S   │    ♣ 10 5
                      └──────┘
              ♠ 7 2
              ♥ A K J 10 9
              ♦ 6 2
              ♣ K J 4 3
```

West leads ♦J. Whatever declarer plays from dummy, the defence can cash two diamond winners, leaving East on lead to play a third diamond winner. If South doesn't ruff the third diamond, East will win the trick.

So South must ruff the diamond. If South ruffs with the ♥9, West overruffs with the ♥Q. Just look: that ♥Q, which could not make a trick in no trumps, has just won a trick! If South realises West has only two diamonds, he can ruff with ♥K and now West must make a trick with the queen, however South plays. The ♥Q has been promoted from a loser to a winner. This is called a trump promotion

This trump promotion happened because:

- Both West and South were out of the same suit.

- East was on lead to play a card in that suit through declarer.

- West had a trump that was nearly but not quite a winner.

- South could ruff high so that West's trump became a winner.

- Or South could ruff low and West could overruff.

How could East know that the trump promotion would work? Of course, he couldn't tell for sure, but it cost him nothing to try. Looking at his hand and dummy, East could see there was no rush to cash other winners. Only a potential trump trick could disappear.

Inexperienced players often cannot see why making the long trump hand ruff could be a winning defence. The last chapter showed one reason, making declarer run out of trumps. Here we see the second reason: a trump trick can be created where there wasn't one before.

The sort of trump holdings where a trump trick can be promoted are:

- Singleton king

- Queen doubleton

- Jack trebleton

- Four to the ten

All these are just one pip short of being a trick in their own right.

Sometimes trump promotions work slightly differently.

```
                    ♥7 6 5
      ♥10 2    [            ]    ♥J 9 3
                    ♥A K Q 8 4
```

Here, if South ruffs with ♥8, West makes his ♥10. And if South ruffs with ♥A or K or Q to avoid the overruff, East has a trump trick with his ♥J. Put out the cards and see it happen.

On this deal West's potential trump trick is the ♥10.

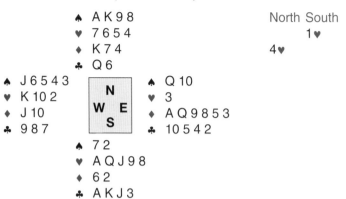

	♠ A K 9 8	North	South
	♥ 7 6 5 4		1♥
	♦ K 7 4	4♥	
	♣ Q 6		

```
♠ J 6 5 4 3          ♠ Q 10
♥ K 10 2      N      ♥ 3
♦ J 10     W     E   ♦ A Q 9 8 5 3
♣ 9 8 7       S      ♣ 10 5 4 2
            ♠ 7 2
            ♥ A Q J 9 8
            ♦ 6 2
            ♣ A K J 3
```

West leads ♦J and three rounds of diamonds are played. South might ruff with ♥9 but West overruffs with ♥10 and waits to win his ♥K.

If South realises West has led a doubleton diamond, he might ruff with ♥J instead of ♥9. If West overruffs with the ♥K, the contract makes because South's ♥A Q will draw West's ♥10 2.

But West need be in no hurry to take his ♥K; it will always make a trick. If West discards a spade instead, he has ♥K 10 2 to South's ♥A J 9 8 and West must make two trump tricks, however South plays. Not overruffing can create an extra trick.

Don't automatically overruff with a certain trump trick.
Wait a while and you may gain an extra trick.

Even if West's hearts were only ♥K 9 2, the suit might be:

```
              ♥7 6 5 4
♥K 9 2      [          ]      ♥10
              ♥A Q J 8 3
```

Not overruffing gains a trick when partner's singleton is ♥10. Put out the cards to check how this particular card magic works.

The uppercut

There is another way to promote a trump trick. Look at this suit.

♥7 6 5 4

♥Q 2   [＿＿＿＿＿]   ♥J 3

♥A K 10 9 8

In the normal course of events, South would lead out ♥A and ♥K and make five heart tricks. But suppose West could lead a suit in which both East and South were void. A ruff by East with ♥J would force an overruff with ♥K. Now West must make ♥Q. This play is called an uppercut. Here is an example.

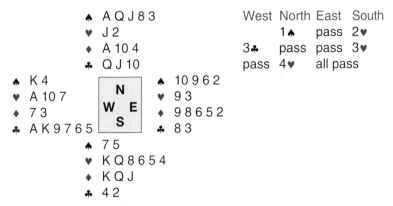

	♠ A Q J 8 3	West	North	East	South
	♥ J 2			1♠	pass 2♥
	♦ A 10 4	3♣	pass	pass	3♥
	♣ Q J 10	pass	4♥	all pass	

♠ K 4
♥ A 10 7
♦ 7 3
♣ A K 9 7 6 5

♠ 10 9 6 2
♥ 9 3
♦ 9 8 6 5 2
♣ 8 3

♠ 7 5
♥ K Q 8 6 5 4
♦ K Q J
♣ 4 2

West leads ♣A and East should play ♣8 to encourage. West continues by cashing ♣K and East completes his signal with ♣3. Dummy has 15 points, South must have at least ten and West has 14. East can have at most one jack. We have no high-card tricks we must cash quickly and ♠K is badly placed. The only hope for a fourth defensive trick is a trump promotion. West leads a third club.

East is going to ruff the club but it costs him nothing to use ♥9 to do so. This is just good enough to force out South's ♥Q and West must now make two heart tricks with his ♥A 10 7, however South plays.

> When ruffing with worthless trumps, always ruff with as high a trump as you can spare.

Here is a slight variation on the last idea:

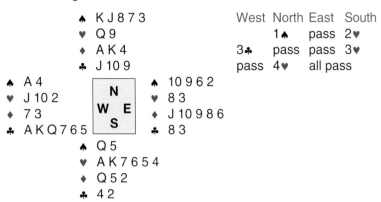

	♠	K J 8 7 3		West	North	East	South
	♥	Q 9				1♠	pass	2♥
	♦	A K 4		3♣	pass	pass	3♥
	♣	J 10 9		pass	4♥	all pass	

West leads ♣A and ♣K, East playing ♣8 then ♣3. Again, East can have few points, and a trump promotion seems to be the defence's best chance. If West plays a third club, East can ruff with ♥8 and force out declarer's ♥K.

If West leads ♣Q, East may not realise that he is meant to ruff. If he discards, the trump promotion is lost and 4♥ makes. West can help his partner defend correctly by leading a small club.

When West leads a low club, East may think that South has ♣Q. East will ruff the club hoping to win the third defensive trick. East may not see why it is necessary, but he should follow the rule of ruffing with the largest trump that can be spared and ruff with ♥8.

The ♥8 forces out declarer's ♥K and West wins a trick with ♥J 10 2.

Try to make the defence easy for partner.

Declarer sometimes has a way of foiling the trump promotion. He can throw away a loser in another suit, rather than overruffing. On the hand above, West should really cash ♠A before playing his third club. Here it didn't matter but it does on the next deal.

Cash all your winners before playing for a trump promotion.

```
♠ Q 5                               West  North  East  South
♥ K 8 6                             pass  pass   3♦    3♠
♦ 7 6 5                             pass  4♠     all pass
♣ K Q 9 4 2
        ┌─────┐   ♠ 7 3
        │  N  │   ♥ 9 7 3
        │W   E│   ♦ A Q J 10 8 4
        │  S  │   ♣ A 8
        └─────┘
```

You, as East, open a rather strong 3♦ third in hand, but opponents still bid to 4♠. West leads ♦K. This means West can only have one or two diamonds. With ♦K x x, the lead would be a small diamond. How should you defend to get declarer one down?

First, overtake ♦K in case it is a singleton and cash ♦Q. Both West and South follow. You have eleven points, dummy has ten, and partner has shown three. South will have most of the remaining 16 points. The best chance to beat 4♠ is a trump promotion. If you play a third diamond, South does not have to ruff. Instead, he could throw his only club (this is a loser-on-loser play) and there is no trump promotion.

Cash ♣A first and beat 4♠ when partner has ♠J 9 2.

Summary

- Extra tricks can be created by a trump promotion, when no other defence is likely to succeed.

- If you get the chance, always overruff with a trump that is not a certain winner. (e.g. Qx or Jxx).

- Don't automatically overruff with a sure trump trick when a second trick might be created, unless you need to get the lead quickly.

- When ruffing from small trumps, use the largest one you can spare.

- Cash any side suit winners before playing to promote a trump.

- Sometimes you must give a ruff and discard to get the trump promotion. Now it is vital to cash all your winners first.

Quiz on trump promotion

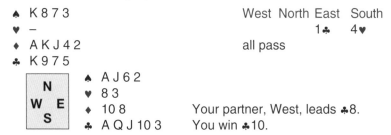

♠ K 8 7 3
♥ –
♦ A K J 4 2
♣ K 9 7 5

West	North	East	South
		1♣	4♥

all pass

♠ A J 6 2
♥ 8 3
♦ 10 8
♣ A Q J 10 3

Your partner, West, leads ♣8.
You win ♣10.

What do you make of the club position? How should you plan to defend?

West has only one or two clubs, with ♣8 6 4 West would lead ♣6, the middle from three. So South must have at least two clubs. It is safe to cash the ♣A. If West shows out, you play ♣Q (a suit preference signal) giving partner a ruff and asking for a spade return.

If West follows to the second club, you must hope that another club will promote a trump trick. But South could discard his losing spade on the club unless you cash ♠A first. Now West's ♥J is the setting trick.

How do you know that ♠A will win? You don't, but if it doesn't how are you going to beat the contract? So you might as well try it.

This is the complete deal:

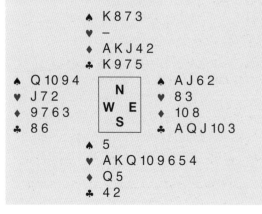

♠ K 8 7 3
♥ –
♦ A K J 4 2
♣ K 9 7 5

♠ Q 10 9 4
♥ J 7 2
♦ 9 7 6 3
♣ 8 6

♠ A J 6 2
♥ 8 3
♦ 10 8
♣ A Q J 10 3

♠ 5
♥ A K Q 10 9 6 5 4
♦ Q 5
♣ 4 2

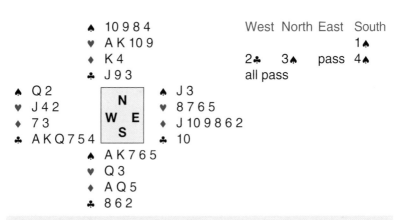

♠ 10 9 8 4
♥ A K 10 9
♦ K 4
♣ J 9 3

West	North	East	South
			1♠
2♣	3♠	pass	4♠
all pass			

♠ Q 2
♥ J 4 2
♦ 7 3
♣ A K Q 7 5 4

♠ J 3
♥ 8 7 6 5
♦ J 10 9 8 6 2
♣ 10

♠ A K 7 6 5
♥ Q 3
♦ A Q 5
♣ 8 6 2

Seeing all four hands, how can the defence beat 4♠ by South?

Play three rounds of clubs. When East discards ♦2 and ♥5, West knows South has no losers to throw if you give a ruff and discard and that a trump promotion is the only hope for the defence. West plays a fourth club. East ruffs with ♠J, promoting a trick for West's ♠Q.

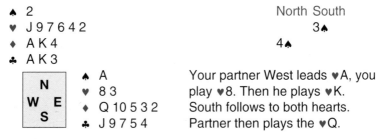

♠ 2
♥ J 9 7 6 4 2
♦ A K 4
♣ A K 3

North	South
	3♠
	4♠

♠ A
♥ 8 3
♦ Q 10 5 3 2
♣ J 9 7 5 4

Your partner West leads ♥A, you play ♥8. Then he plays ♥K. South follows to both hearts. Partner then plays the ♥Q.

What is partner doing? What card do you play?

Partner is trying to promote a trump trick. He would have led a small heart to help you, but he doesn't have one! You must ruff with ♠A, even though it is a sure trump trick. That is one trump trick.

The defence will now make a second trump trick if partner has Qx or Jxx or 10xxx. If you don't ruff, declarer will ruff the heart, cross to dummy and play a spade. Your ♠A will win but if partner has one of the holdings described, declarer can now draw partner's trumps.

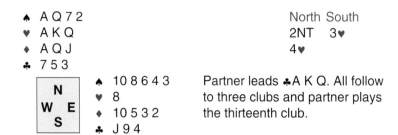

♠ A Q 7 2
♥ A K Q
♦ A Q J
♣ 7 5 3

North	South
2NT	3♥
	4♥

♠ 10 8 6 4 3
♥ 8
♦ 10 5 3 2
♣ J 9 4

Partner leads ♣A K Q. All follow to three clubs and partner plays the thirteenth club.

What is partner doing? When will his play work?

Partner is trying to promote a trump for the defence. For this to work partner must have four hearts. If his hearts are headed by ♥J, partner always has a heart trick. If partner has ♥10 and ♥9, your ♥8 will force out declarer's ♥J and promote a trump trick for one down.

♠ 7 2
♥ A K Q J 8
♦ 9 6
♣ K J 10 3

West	North	East	South
			1♠
3♦	3♥	pass	3♠
pass	4♠	all pass	

♠ A 8 6 4
♥ 4
♦ A K Q 5 3 2
♣ 9 2

You are West. You lead ♦A and ♦K. Partner plays ♦4 then ♦5, declarer plays ♦7 then ♦8.

How do you defend?

Partner has three diamonds and probably no points. There can be no outside tricks to cash, so a ruff and discard won't matter. We must try a trump promotion. Play a third diamond, giving a ruff and discard (see page 92), which rarely works in defence – this is an exception! It is ruffed in dummy. Win ♠A straight away and play a fourth diamond. If partner can ruff this with the nine or ten, your ♠8 will become a trick. You hope spades are distributed something like:

```
                  ♠7 2
    ♠A 8 6 4    [            ]    ♠9 5
                  ♠K Q J 10 3
```

15 leads to a slam

Normal lead rules don't apply against slams.

When opponents bid to the six level, WE don't lead to set up long suit winners. To beat the contract, WE just have to find two tricks.

The lead should be chosen to:

- Cash two aces. Blackwood often stops this happening, of course – but it does happen…

- Cash an ace king holding in a side suit.

- Establish a high card trick straight away.

- Give or get a ruff.

- Give nothing away.

This chapter is a quiz to see if you can work out how to apply the rules above. It should help you beat lots of slams.

What lead do you make?

♠	J 10 9 2	North	South
♥	A 8 4	1♣	2♠
♦	6 4 2	3♠	4NT
♣	10 9 8	5♦	6♠

Lead ♥A. Opponents don't know trumps break badly and you have a spade trick. Make sure your other trick doesn't disappear. Cash your ace. Declarer might be able to discard heart losers on clubs or diamonds

♠	A 2	North	South
♥	J 8 4	1♣	2♠
♦	6 4 2	3♠	4♣
♣	10 9 8 7 6	4♠	6♠

It is not clear what South's 4♣ shows but it is probably a useful high card in opener's suit. Lead ♣10. If partner follows to the club, win ♠A straightaway and play another club, hoping that partner can ruff.

♠ 6 2		West	North	East	South
♥ J 8 4			1♣	pass	2♠
♦ A 4 2		pass	3♠	pass	4♣
♣ 10 9 6 5 2		pass	4♠	pass	6♠
		pass	pass	dble	all pass

Doubling a slam contract asks partner to find an unusual lead. It is sometimes called a Lightner double. Often the doubler is trying to get a ruff and you have to guess in which suit partner has a void. It looks most likely to be a club. Tell partner about your entry by leading ♣2 – a low card asking for a low suit.

♠ A 3 2		North	South
♥ K Q 4		1♣	4NT
♦ 6 4 2		5♦	6NT
♣ 10 9 8 6			

Never mind why opponents have bid like this, some people do! Lead ♥K and hope they need a spade trick to make their contract. You will win ♠A as soon as spades are led and cash your heart trick.

♠ Q J 10		North	South
♥ 8 4		1♣	2♥
♦ Q 10 9 8 6		3♣	3NT
♣ 10 9 8		4NT	6NT

Against 3NT you lead ♦10 but against a slam, your spade sequence is a much better lead, not giving away unnecessary tricks. Try ♠Q.

♠ Q 10 2		North	South
♥ 8 6 3 2		1♣	2♠
♦ Q 10 9 8		3♣	3NT
♣ Q 10		4NT	6NT

You would lead ♦10 against 3NT but prefer ♥6 against 6NT or 7NT – give nothing away. Opponents usually have at least 33 points when they bid a no trump slam. You have six points, partner probably has nothing so leading a heart should not kill an honour in partner's hand.

♠ Q 10 2		North	South
♥ 8 6 3			
♦ Q 10 8		1♣	2♥
♣ J 9 7 4		3♥	4NT
		5♥	6♥

Normally, you try to avoid a trump lead against a slam in case you catch partner's ♥Q. But broken holdings in the other suits mean that non-trump leads look dangerous and ♥3 gives nothing away.

♠ Q 10 2		North	South
♥ 8 6			
♦ Q J 9 8		1♣	2♥
♣ J 9 7 4		3♥	4NT
		5♥	6♥

You only have to make the diamonds in the above hand a touch better. Now ♦Q looks to be the best lead, rather than your doubleton trump.

♠ A 10 6 4		North	South
♥ 8			
♦ J 9 8		1♣	2♥
♣ J 9 7 4		3♥	4NT
		5♥	6♥

Lead ♠A. Partner might have ♠K; it's not unknown for opponents to be missing an ace and king in a side suit. Winning ♠A stops a spade loser being discarded and partner might have a trump trick to come.

Summary

- In 6NT, opponents usually have at least 33 points between them.

- Try to give nothing away on the lead.

- Choose a 3+ card sequence or an ace king suit if you have one.

- Lead a singleton if partner could have either that ace or the trump ace. If you have an ace and Blackwood was used, don't lead your singleton as they should not be short of two aces!

- With a likely trump trick, cash your ace at trick one.

- Lead an ace far more often than you do against a low-level contract.

- If partner doubles, make an unusual lead, often to give a ruff.

16 planning the defence

Defenders can plan too

Defenders win tricks in just the same way as declarer but there are some significant differences.

- The good news is that WE don't have to win as many tricks as declarer does.

- WE get to fire the first shot in the battle with the opening lead. It can tell partner a lot about our hand.

- The bad news is that each partner can only see half of the joint resources so WE have to:

communicate clearly to collaborate successfully.

To be successful, declarer has to make a cunning plan. The defenders must do the same. When you see dummy, ask yourself:

1) How many tricks do WE need to defeat the contract?

2) Based on the bidding and what you can see in dummy, how is declarer likely to play this hand?

3) If you are third in hand, what can you tell from the opening lead? Is it the opening lead you would have expected? If not, what does that suggest?

4) What else do you know about partner's hand? Did he bid? How many points might he hold?

5) How many tricks will my hand probably yield?

6) What must partner hold to produce the extra tricks WE need?

Make your plan to get declarer one down.

Let's look at an example in detail to see how the planning process works. You are East.

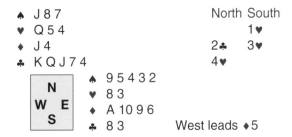

	♠ J 8 7		North	South
	♥ Q 5 4			1♥
	♦ J 4		2♣	3♥
	♣ K Q J 7 4		4♥	

N W E S

♠ 9 5 4 3 2
♥ 8 3
♦ A 10 9 6
♣ 8 3   West leads ♦5

1) WE need to find four tricks to defeat the contract.

2) Declarer will probably draw trumps and run the club suit.

3) West probably has four or five diamonds to an honour, maybe ♦K.

4) West didn't bid. South probably has about 16HCP and there are ten points in dummy so West has about ten points. South's bidding showed six hearts so West has two trumps at most.

5) Your hand has one trick – ♦A. If West has ♦K, that's two. No more diamond tricks can be made as dummy only has two.

6) WE need two more tricks from a spade, a trump or the ♣A.

Using the clues, you can deduce that West might have any of the following hands:

♠ A Q 6	or	♠ K 10 6	or	♠ 10 6
♥ 7 6		♥ 7 6		♥ K 7
♦ K 8 7 5 2		♦ K 8 7 5 2		♦ K 8 7 5 2
♣ 9 6 5		♣ A 6 5		♣ A 6 5 2

If West has ♥K or ♣A he can take them later, along with his ♦K. There is no need to grab them this minute. If West has ♠K or ♠A Q, he needs your help now to set up spade tricks, because you are not going to gain the lead again. If you return a diamond West won't be able to lead spades without giving a vital trick away. Declarer might then have time to throw losing spades away on the clubs.

Conclusion: you must play a spade at trick two.

You do not know that West has spade tricks but can work out that he might. If he does, a spade switch is imperative. If West hasn't any spade tricks, the switch does no harm. Perhaps the full deal is:

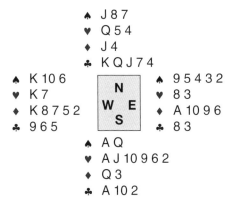

```
                ♠ J 8 7
                ♥ Q 5 4
                ♦ J 4
                ♣ K Q J 7 4
  ♠ K 10 6                      ♠ 9 5 4 3 2
  ♥ K 7         ┌─────────┐     ♥ 8 3
  ♦ K 8 7 5 2   │   N     │     ♦ A 10 9 6
  ♣ 9 6 5       │ W   E   │     ♣ 8 3
                │   S     │
                └─────────┘
                ♠ A Q
                ♥ A J 10 9 6 2
                ♦ Q 3
                ♣ A 10 2
```

> When switching, lead a suit where partner might hold some high cards.

What should you do at trick two on this deal? Again, you are East.

```
   ♠ A K 7                North  South
   ♥ J 7 6 2                       1♥
   ♦ Q 8 4                3♥       4♥
   ♣ 8 7 4
              ┌─────────┐ ♠ J 9 5 4
              │   N     │ ♥ 3
              │ W   E   │ ♦ A K 9 2
              │   S     │ ♣ Q 10 9 2
              └─────────┘
```

West leads ♦5, to ♦4, ♦K and ♦3. From the Rule of Eleven, you can work out that declarer has one diamond left, but if ♦A is cashed now, a winner is set up in dummy for a discard. A switch is needed at trick two, but what should you lead?

A club up to weakness is best, but play ♣10, not ♣2, in case declarer ducks the club round to dummy's ♣8.

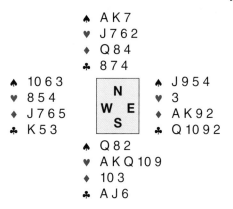

```
              ♠ A K 7
              ♥ J 7 6 2
              ♦ Q 8 4
              ♣ 8 7 4
♠ 10 6 3                        ♠ J 9 5 4
♥ 8 5 4          N              ♥ 3
♦ J 7 6 5    W     E            ♦ A K 9 2
♣ K 5 3          S              ♣ Q 10 9 2
              ♠ Q 8 2
              ♥ A K Q 10 9
              ♦ 10 3
              ♣ A J 6
```

Lead up to weakness in dummy.

This deal catches out many bridge players when it is set as a problem.

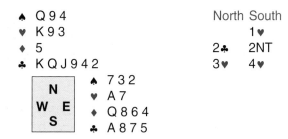

```
              ♠ Q 9 4              North   South
              ♥ K 9 3                       1♥
              ♦ 5                   2♣      2NT
              ♣ K Q J 9 4 2        3♥      4♥
                       ♠ 7 3 2
              N        ♥ A 7
          W     E      ♦ Q 8 6 4
              S        ♣ A 8 7 5
```

WE need four tricks to defeat the contract. Given time, declarer will draw trumps and cash his clubs, plenty of discards for all his losers.

Partner, West, leads ♣3. It is unusual to lead a suit they have bid. A moment's thought shows what partner is up to. When declarer follows with ♣6, the lead is obviously a singleton. If partner had started with ♣10 3, he would have led ♣10.

South's 2NT shows 15–16 and the 4♥ bid confirms a 5-card heart suit. That means partner has about four points and three trumps.

How do you plan to defend?

You can see three tricks, ♣A, ♥A and the club ruff. But where is the fourth trick coming from? Possibly ♦A or ♠A, but what if partner only has ♠K? Having ruffed the club, partner won't be able to play a spade without giving a trick away.

Switch to a spade at trick two. The club ruff can wait. As you have ♥A, you are bound to get in before declarer can draw partner's trumps.

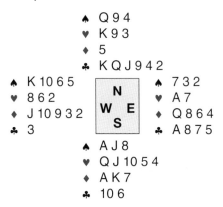

```
              ♠ Q 9 4
              ♥ K 9 3
              ♦ 5
              ♣ K Q J 9 4 2
♠ K 10 6 5                  ♠ 7 3 2
♥ 8 6 2          N          ♥ A 7
♦ J 10 9 3 2   W   E        ♦ Q 8 6 4
♣ 3              S          ♣ A 8 7 5
              ♠ A J 8
              ♥ Q J 10 5 4
              ♦ A K 7
              ♣ 10 6
```

If ♥K and ♥A were swapped round, it would still be right to play a spade at trick two. From the bidding you know partner has three trumps and the ruff can wait till you get in with a trump.

Misleading declarer

For most players it is quite enough to try and find the best defence. But there is one other weapon in your defensive armoury that hasn't been mentioned and that is deceit.

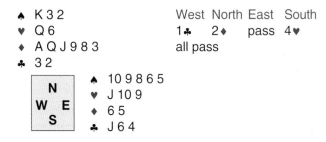

```
♠ K 3 2          West   North  East   South
♥ Q 6            1♣     2♦     pass   4♥
♦ A Q J 9 8 3    all pass
♣ 3 2
          N          ♠ 10 9 8 6 5
        W   E        ♥ J 10 9
          S          ♦ 6 5
                     ♣ J 6 4
```

West leads ♣A against 4♥. As East, try to beat the contract.

Prospects are not good. Two clubs and the ♠A perhaps. South's jump to 4♥ combined with our holding of ♥J 10 9 and dummy's ♥Q 6 means that South's hearts are ♥A K heading a seven or eight card suit.

Where could another trick possibly come from? Not diamonds even if partner has ♦K. Only one spade, as dummy has ♠K. Trumps seem to offer the only chance but ♥J 10 9 are not a winning holding.

Perhaps you could fool declarer into thinking there is a trump promotion available. Play ♣J, then ♣4, high-low, pretending you have only two clubs. Partner might just cash ♠A and then play a third club. And perhaps declarer will ruff with dummy's ♥Q. Now your ♥J 10 9 will win a trick. A wonderful swindle when the contract was laydown!

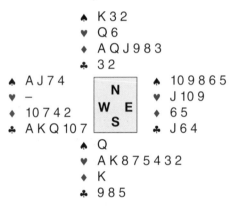

```
              ♠ K 3 2
              ♥ Q 6
              ♦ A Q J 9 8 3
              ♣ 3 2
♠ A J 7 4          N        ♠ 10 9 8 6 5
♥ –                        ♥ J 10 9
♦ 10 7 4 2    W     E       ♦ 6 5
♣ A K Q 10 7      S        ♣ J 6 4
              ♠ Q
              ♥ A K 8 7 5 4 3 2
              ♦ K
              ♣ 9 8 5
```

It will never happen, you say. Look at this deal:

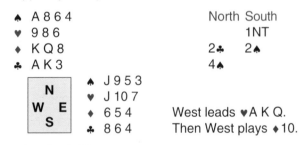

```
              ♠ A 8 6 4              North  South
              ♥ 9 8 6                        1NT
              ♦ K Q 8               2♣    2♠
              ♣ A K 3               4♠
      N        ♠ J 9 5 3
              ♥ J 10 7
  W     E      ♦ 6 5 4            West leads ♥A K Q.
      S        ♣ 8 6 4            Then West plays ♦10.
```

Where is your fourth trick?

The spade suit breaks 4-1, probably

$$\spadesuit A\,8\,6\,4$$

$$\spadesuit 2 \qquad \boxed{} \quad \spadesuit J\,9\,5\,3$$

$$\spadesuit K\,Q\,10\,7$$

Left to his own devices, South will cash the ♠K and then lead small to dummy's ♠A. This is the correct play, as it allows South to pick up ♠J 9 5 3 in your hand. If partner had four spades to the jack there is nothing South can do. West always has a trump trick.

If South is a good player he will get this right. How can you stop him making the correct play?

Drop your ♠9 under declarer's ♠K. Now declarer can safely play the spades another way and, because of your ♠9, he will probably cash ♠Q next as he can pick up ♠J 5 3 2 in the West hand.

This is a well-known position, often called an obligatory false card. But most declarers won't expect an innocent-looking player like you to know about it!

Summary

- Setting up long suits is rarely useful against a suit contract. Only continue the suit partner led when to switch would help declarer.

- Work out where the defensive tricks are coming from and whether they will need setting up quickly.

- Defensive tricks must be cashed before declarer can discard them.

- Lead up to weakness in the dummy if switching to a new suit.

- Lead through declarer's strength, when you have nothing in the suit.

- When either defender wins an early trick, the sight of dummy, plus the bidding, should help them formulate the defensive plan.

- If you can give partner a ruff, you don't necessarily have to do it straight away if you have a quick trump entry.

- If all else fails, try to deceive declarer.

Quiz on planning the defence

♠ Q 9 8 4
♥ 10 9 3
♦ 5
♣ K Q 9 4 2

	West	North	East	South
			1♠	3♥
	pass	4♥	all pass	

♠ A J 10 7 3 2
♥ A 7
♦ K 8 6 4   You are East.
♣ J   West leads ♠5.

How many tricks do WE need to beat the contract?

WE need to find four tricks.

How is declarer likely to play this hand?

He might draw trumps and cash his winners or he might need to ruff a diamond or two in dummy first.

What can you tell from the opening lead?

Partner has led ♠5, dummy played ♠4, you played ♠A and declarer ♠6. Partner must have a singleton as with ♠K 5 he would lead the ♠K.

What other information is there?

South's 3♥ jump overcall shows a good 6-card suit and 12+ points. Partner probably has few points as he showed no interest in the opening bid and, of course, we have deduced he has a singleton spade.

Where are those four tricks coming from?

♠A, a spade ruff and ♥A are only three tricks. WE need one more. ♦K won't make a trick since dummy has a singleton and South is favourite to hold ♦A.

The best chance of an extra trick is a club ruff. But declarer will draw trumps before playing on clubs; he won't help you get a ruff. The answer is to play a club at trick two. Declarer wins and plays a trump. You win the heart and give partner a spade ruff. Do this by playing ♠2, a suit preference signal for clubs.

case studies

We have now looked at all the elements of defence in detail. What matters is putting all these new ideas into practice at the bridge table.

To help you do this, the book finishes with twelve case studies. Each takes a look at a real hand and step by step takes you through a series of questions about the defence to put the principles into practice.

Sometimes you will be West and have to make the opening lead.

Sometimes you will be East and for you the problem starts when the lead is made and dummy goes down. Make sure you know who you are on each deal; the first hand diagram should help you.

The first question in each case study is something like:

What are your first thoughts?

Take this opportunity to:

- Review the bidding, what happened and also what didn't happen.

- Assess how many points each player is likely to have.

- Work out what the lead tells you about partner's hand.

- Decide what the bidding and lead tell you about the distribution.

- Make a plan for the defence, using the information you have.

A discussion of the answer follows and you learn a bit more before the next question. The new information may change the defensive plan.

When you tire of problems on paper, have your friends round for a real game of bridge. You may like the *Really Easy Practice* series, which provides good hands to play and a commentary on what you might have done.

Case study 1

♠	10 8	North South
♥	J 6 4	1NT
♦	A Q J 7 6 5	3NT
♣	A 4	

```
    N
  W   E
    S
```

♠ Q 7 4
♥ A 9 8 5
♦ 10 4   Partner leads ♠6.
♣ K 9 8 3   Dummy plays ♠8.

You are East. What are your thoughts on seeing dummy?

South has 12–14 points, North has 12, you have nine, so partner will have about six points. Points are not so important when North's good diamond suit will produce six tricks for declarer.

Partner has at least four and possibly five spades. From ♠6 lead, a low card, you can tell he should have at least one spade honour.

Which card should you play?

Third hand plays high. Put your ♠Q on dummy's ♠8 to give your side the best chance of either winning the trick or setting up winners to cash. Declarer wins ♠Q with ♠K, plays ♦2 to ♦Q in dummy and leads ♥J.

Can you see any hope for the defence?

Declarer has six diamonds for certain. Even if West does hold ♦K, declarer can finesse it. With one spade already made and ♣A that you can see in dummy that makes eight tricks.

Partner led ♠6. Use the Rule of Eleven, 11 − 6 = 5, so there are five cards higher than the six between dummy, your hand and declarer's hand. You can see four cards higher than the six – dummy has the ♠10 8 and you have the ♠Q 7. Declarer played ♠K at trick one. He cannot have another spade stopper. Partner has a holding like ♠A J 9 6 x.

So how should you defend?

If you allow declarer to make even one heart trick, he has made his contract. Go up with ♥A and lead ♠7.

If declarer had cashed six rounds of diamonds instead of playing a heart, what four cards would you have discarded from your hand?

If South cashes the six diamonds first, East must discard to help partner, as you must stop him throwing a spade away. Discard ♥9 first to show a good heart card, then ♣9 to show a club honour. Follow these up with ♣3 and ♥5 to confirm the two peters. High cards then low let partner know it is safe to throw away in those suits. West should throw two hearts and then a club, trusting partner's discards.

```
              ♠ 10 8
              ♥ J 6 4
              ♦ A Q J 7 6 5
              ♣ A 4
♠ A J 9 6 3   ┌─────────┐   ♠ Q 7 4
♥ 10 2        │   N     │   ♥ A 9 8 5
♦ 9 3 2       │ W   E   │   ♦ 10 4
♣ J 10 5      │   S     │   ♣ K 9 8 3
              └─────────┘
              ♠ K 5 2
              ♥ K Q 7 3
              ♦ K 8
              ♣ Q 7 6 2
```

What lessons can we learn from the deal?

Declarer made a good try for the contract by playing a heart early. It would be all too easy for East to play low without thinking, hoping that declarer was going to take a losing finesse.

Always use the Rule of Eleven when partner leads fourth highest. At trick one say to yourself, 11 − 6 = 5. You can see two in dummy and two in hand. Declarer has only one card to beat ♠6. When declarer wins ♠K, you know he has only small cards left. When a heart is led from dummy, whether it is ♥J or ♥4, you should be ready to leap up with your ♥A and play a spade.

Case study 2

♠ 9 5
♥ K 10 8 7 5
♦ 3
♣ K 10 7 6 4

South bids 1NT and North raises to 3NT. You are West, on lead with this hand.

Should you try a heart or a club?

South has a balanced 12–14 points but North need not be balanced since 3NT might be based on a long minor suit and no more than 12 points. It is reasonable to hope partner has a few points but certainly no more than ten. It is unlikely North has a 4-card major, as Stayman was not used, but South could have one or both majors.

Either clubs or hearts could be the right lead. But without second sight, you should choose a heart – both because it is an unbid major and because the heart pips are that little bit better, 8 7 5 as opposed to 7 6 4!

Which heart card do you lead?

Your fourth highest is normal, so lead ♥7. Dummy goes down:

```
            ♠ Q 10 4
            ♥ Q 9
            ♦ A K 10 7 4
            ♣ Q J 2
♠ 9 5
♥ K 10 8 7 5      N
♦ 3           W       E
♣ K 10 7 6 4      S
```

Trick one goes ♥7, ♥9, ♥A, and ♥2. Having won the ace, partner returns ♥3 and declarer plays ♥4.

What do you make of the heart position? Do you win trick two with your ♥K or do you duck to keep communication with partner?

Partner can't have the ♥J; he would have played it at trick one. Partner has returned the lowest outstanding heart but he can't have four hearts since South still has the ♥J. South must hold ♥J 6 4 2.

So hearts are divided:

♥Q 9

♥K 10 8 7 5 ░░░░░░░░░░░ ♥A 3

♥J 6 4 2

Don't duck. Declarer would still have a heart stop. South still has
♥J 6. Win the ♥K at trick two and play ♥8 to drive out South's ♥J.
This lower card is a suit preference signal and asks for clubs.

Look at the complete deal. Declarer had three spades, one heart,
three diamonds and one club. If there were a 3-3 or 4-2 diamond
break there would be no problem as declarer can happily lose the
lead to East.

As diamonds break so badly, declarer has to try the club finesse
for his ninth trick, thus losing four hearts and a club for one down.

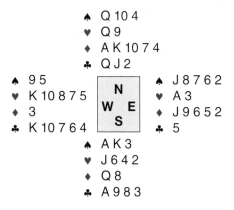

♠ Q 10 4
♥ Q 9
♦ A K 10 7 4
♣ Q J 2

♠ 9 5
♥ K 10 8 7 5
♦ 3
♣ K 10 7 6 4

♠ J 8 7 6 2
♥ A 3
♦ J 9 6 5 2
♣ 5

♠ A K 3
♥ J 6 4 2
♦ Q 8
♣ A 9 8 3

What lessons can we learn from the deal?

3NT was a good contract. If West had followed to a second diamond,
declarer could have played ♦10 from dummy on the second round of
diamonds, prepared to lose the trick to the safe hand.

West found the best lead, but must watch the pips on the small
cards in hearts. To exit with ♥5 would give declarer an extra trick.

East should watch for a signal, although he might have difficulty
recognising ♥8 as a low card. ♥10, asking for a spade would be
easier to read. In fact, it doesn't matter on this deal. East must
throw a spade on the third heart, keeping the same diamond
length as dummy.

Case study 3

```
♠ A Q J 4 3
♥ K 5
♦ 9 8 7
♣ 7 5 3
```

	N	
W		E
	S	

```
♠ 10 9 6 2
♥ 4 3 2
♦ A 3
♣ 8 6 4 2
```

West	North	East	South
			1♦
1♥	1♠	pass	1NT
pass	3NT	all pass	

Partner leads ♥Q.
It is ducked in both
hands.

You are East. What are your first thoughts?

Declarer has 15–16 points for a 1NT rebid, dummy has ten,
leaving 10–11 for partner. Declarer must have three hearts to
duck the first trick, so partner has QJ10xx.

To beat this contract WE must set up and cash our heart winners
before declarer can take nine tricks. Declarer may make five
spades but my four spades will stop the suit if partner has ♠K.

Play ♥2 at trick one with no useful heart cards. Partner continues
with ♥8, which is won by dummy's ♥K.

Is there any significance in ♥8 rather than ♥J?

It looks like partner has ♥Q J 10 9 8 and is trying to show a
possible club entry with a suit preference signal. At trick three
dummy leads ♦9 .

Can you see any way the contract might be beaten?

Declarer is setting up diamonds. You have to hope that declarer
has two diamond losers. You must win the first diamond to play
your last heart and set up the heart winners for partner.

Partner will then be able to win the second diamond trick to cash
those winners. It's one of the times second hand must play high.
You must protect partner's entry by winning ♦A and playing your
last heart.

The complete deal is

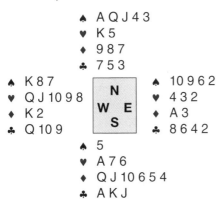

```
              ♠ A Q J 4 3
              ♥ K 5
              ♦ 9 8 7
              ♣ 7 5 3
♠ K 8 7                        ♠ 10 9 6 2
♥ Q J 10 9 8    N              ♥ 4 3 2
♦ K 2         W   E            ♦ A 3
♣ Q 10 9        S              ♣ 8 6 4 2
              ♠ 5
              ♥ A 7 6
              ♦ Q J 10 6 5 4
              ♣ A K J
```

What lessons do we learn from the deal?

Second hand plays low is a good general rule, but we must not fall asleep and stop thinking. It is too easy to lazily follow with ♦3.

If you do play low, partner can win the ♦K and clear the heart suit. But you don't have another heart to lead when you win the ♦A. Sadly, partner's club entry is too slow and declarer has his winners set up before WE can cash ours.

Imagine the two diamond honours are swapped round, so that East has ♦K 3 and West has ♦A 2. It is still just as important for East to win the first diamond trick, but it is a lot harder to go up with the king on the first round.

When you think about it, the play of the king is very unlikely to cost (unless South has an unlikely 7-card suit and partner the singleton ace). To play ♦K from ♦K 3 would be considered quite an expert play. But once you have seen the idea in action, it may occur to you when this defensive position arises on a future occasion.

Case study 4

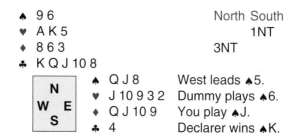

```
♠ 9 6                          North  South
♥ A K 5                               1NT
♦ 8 6 3                        3NT
♣ K Q J 10 8
```

N	♠ Q J 8	West leads ♠5.
W E	♥ J 10 9 3 2	Dummy plays ♠6.
S	♦ Q J 10 9	You play ♠J.
	♣ 4	Declarer wins ♠K.

You are East. What are your first thoughts?

Declarer has 12–14, dummy has 13 and you have seven points. That leaves about seven for partner.

One spade, two hearts, two diamonds and four clubs makes nine tricks. Have we any defence? Declarer plays ♣3 to dummy's ♣10 and then leads ♣K. It looks like partner has ♣A.

What holding could partner have in spades?

Partner led ♠5. If you use the Rule of Eleven, 11 − 5 = 6, there are six cards higher than the five in the other three hands. Dummy has two, you have three and declarer has played the ♠K at trick one.

That means declarer has no card higher than the ♠5 in his hand and partner must have ♠A 10 7 5 and maybe one or two more.

WE have all the high spades, how can you let partner know?

First of all, let's think about what you should discard on the club. You could safely throw ♥2, which suggests that you don't want a heart and do want a diamond. You know that declarer must have nine tricks unless WE can cash four spade tricks now. But partner does not know that, only you do.

How can you pass the message to partner?

Discard ♠Q. That will wake partner up! Partner should realise that all his spades are winners and he had better cash them quickly.

Here is the full deal:

```
                ♠ 9 6
                ♥ A K 5
                ♦ 8 6 3
                ♣ K Q J 10 8
  ♠ A 10 7 5 3        ♠ Q J 8
  ♥ 6 4          N    ♥ J 10 9 3 2
  ♦ 5 4 2     W   E   ♦ Q J 10 9
  ♣ A 6 2        S    ♣ 4
                ♠ K 4 2
                ♥ Q 8 7
                ♦ A K 7
                ♣ 9 7 5 3
```

What lessons can we learn from the deal?

Always try to work out what values partner could hold. There is no point in playing for the impossible. No trump auctions in particular often put quite precise point counts on the opposition hands. It is fairly simple arithmetic to work out how many points partner might have.

The Rule of Eleven works well here – apply it whenever partner leads what looks like a fourth highest card. It only takes a couple of seconds and every now and again the answer will surprise you.

Having worked out how to beat the contract, you have to find a way to pass the message to partner. Without any clues, partner would win ♣A and would probably try to find a way to put you on lead. If you had discarded ♥2, he would probably play a diamond.

Once you think of ♠Q discard, it is obviously the best answer. So take your time over the crucial discard – the answer may not occur to you straight away. If your hand had been different, say:

♠ J 8 2
♥ 10 9 8 3 2
♦ A 9 7 4
♣ 4

you would discard ♦9 at the first opportunity to show your ♦A as an entry card, so that partner could put you in for a spade lead through declarer's spade holding.

Case study 5

You are West and hold

♠	J 9 7 6
♥	10 9 8
♦	5 4 3
♣	6 4 2

North	South
	pass
1♠	2NT
3NT	

What do you lead to 3NT?

2NT shows 10–11 points as South has passed originally. So North has a minimum of 15. You have one, leaving partner with up to 13–14 points. Don't lead spades when North has shown 4+ spades. Hearts looks the best lead as the pips are better and hearts is the unbid major. Lead ♥10.

```
              ♠  A Q 10 4
              ♥  J 5 3
              ♦  K J 6
              ♣  A 9 7
♠  J 9 7 6        N
♥  10 9 8      W     E
♦  5 4 3          S
♣  6 4 2
```

To your surprise, the ♥10 holds the trick and partner plays ♥7.

What do you make of it so far? What now?

♥7 is encouraging: partner presumably has four hearts. Lead ♥9. This holds too, partner playing the ♥6. Lead your third heart to partner's ♥Q and declarer's ♥A. Declarer now plays ♣Q. Partner wins ♣K, cashes ♥K, spades are discarded by dummy and declarer.

What do you discard?

A club. As declarer has already set up his winners in clubs this gives nothing away. Partner exits with a club. If partner had ♦A, he would cash it to get declarer down; so declarer has ♦A. Declarer started with four clubs and now cashes his two clubs.

What discards do you make on the club winners?

Declarer has one spade, one heart, two diamonds and three club tricks. He must find ♦Q for his contract. If declarer has ♦10, he can play either hand for ♦Q. If you throw all your diamonds away, it will be easy for declarer to guess to play partner for ♦Q.

You must protect partner's ♦Q by hanging on to your little diamonds. Spades are your only cards of value, but you can discard two since you know partner has ♠K. You must hope partner throws a spade on the fourth club.

The complete deal was:

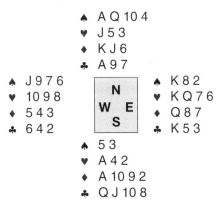

```
              ♠ A Q 10 4
              ♥ J 5 3
              ♦ K J 6
              ♣ A 9 7
♠ J 9 7 6                     ♠ K 8 2
♥ 10 9 8         N            ♥ K Q 7 6
♦ 5 4 3      W     E          ♦ Q 8 7
♣ 6 4 2          S            ♣ K 5 3
              ♠ 5 3
              ♥ A 4 2
              ♦ A 10 9 2
              ♣ Q J 10 8
```

What lessons do we learn from the deal?

If West throws spades, this should be the end position with only spades and diamonds left:

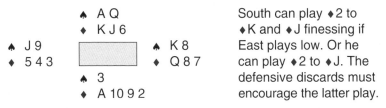

```
              ♠ A Q
              ♦ K J 6
♠ J 9                        ♠ K 8
♦ 5 4 3                      ♦ Q 8 7
              ♠ 3
              ♦ A 10 9 2
```

South can play ♦2 to ♦K and ♦J finessing if East plays low. Or he can play ♦2 to ♦J. The defensive discards must encourage the latter play.

Many Wests would hang on to their spades, the only cards of value. It is hard to spot that ♦5 4 3 have a role to play.

Discard to protect partner's high cards.

Case study 6

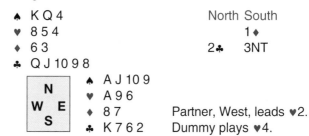

♠ K Q 4
♥ 8 5 4
♦ 6 3
♣ Q J 10 9 8

♠ A J 10 9
♥ A 9 6
♦ 8 7
♣ K 7 6 2

North	South
	1♦
2♣	3NT

Partner, West, leads ♥2.
Dummy plays ♥4.

What are your thoughts? Do you play ♥A to trick one?

Dummy, with eight points, is a minimum for his 2♣ bid. Declarer has shown 17–19 and you hold 12 points. Partner can have at most three points so it is very unlikely WE can cash four heart tricks straight away.

The 1♦ opening shows 4+ cards. As you and dummy have only two diamonds each, partner may stop diamonds. Partner has four hearts, so declarer has three. Declarer's most likely shape is 3343 or 3352.

There seems to be no reason to play anything but the ♥A at trick one but do not automatically return the ♥9.

It looks like declarer will need the clubs. Can he bring the suit in?

Declarer must have ♣A. He can cross to dummy with a spade and take the club finesse. But because you hold four clubs the winning finesse will only generate one or two extra tricks.

Declarer might forgo the club finesse; after all he doesn't even know it will win. Instead, he might play ♣A and another club, giving you your club trick. He then has the spade entry to cash the club winners. That seems a more likely line of play.

Is there anything you can do to foil his plans?

You will beat the contract if you can remove dummy's spade entry before the clubs are set up. Playing ♠A and another spade might work, if declarer has only two spades. But look what happens if you play ♠J. Declarer has to win with a high spade in dummy and the entry has gone.

Here is the complete deal:

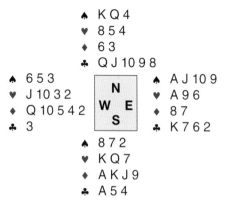

                ♠ K Q 4
                ♥ 8 5 4
                ♦ 6 3
                ♣ Q J 10 9 8
    ♠ 6 5 3   ♠ A J 10 9
    ♥ J 10 3 2   N   ♥ A 9 6
    ♦ Q 10 5 4 2 W   E   ♦ 8 7
    ♣ 3   S   ♣ K 7 6 2
                ♠ 8 7 2
                ♥ K Q 7
                ♦ A K J 9
                ♣ A 5 4

What lessons do we learn from this deal?

West is quite right to lead a heart, even though his diamond suit is longer and stronger. South opened 1♦ and East cannot have length in diamonds too. West is also right to lead a fourth highest heart against no trumps, rather than the ♥J since he has only got two heart honours.

Always stop and think at trick one. It is normal to return partner's lead when you win the first trick, but it is not always right.

Look what happens if you return a heart. Declarer wins and plays the ♣A and another club. You win and play your third heart. Declarer wins and plays a spade towards dummy. You can take your ace but then what? Declarer has one spade, two hearts, two diamonds and four clubs.

Whether you are declarer or defender, it is exactly the same. It is not enough to set up winners; there must be an entry to cash them. If dummy has a long suit that will provide a lot of tricks, always check whether dummy has an entry and whether, as here, you can remove that entry prematurely. Look back to page 50 on removing dummy's entry.

Equally, when setting up winners for the defence, it is vital that the hand with the winners has an entry to cash them, or the winners are useless.

Case study 7

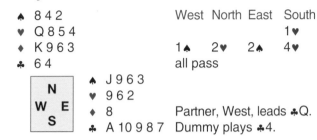

```
        ♠ 842                     West  North East  South
        ♥ Q854                                          1♥
        ♦ K963                    1♠    2♥    2♠    4♥
        ♣ 64                      all pass
              ♠ J963
        N     ♥ 962
      W   E   ♦ 8          Partner, West, leads ♣Q.
        S     ♣ A10987     Dummy plays ♣4.
```

What are your first thoughts? What do you make of the lead?

You can see ten points. Declarer has perhaps 16–18 points but that still leaves about 13 for partner.

Why hasn't partner led a spade? Surely, with the ♠AK or ♠KQ partner would have tried a spade first. Presumably partner has an unattractive spade holding, say ♠Axxxx or more likely ♠AQxxx. If partner has five spades headed by the ace, WE have at most one spade trick to take.

Could ♣Q be a singleton? It is possible. It would give declarer ♣KJ532. But partner probably only has one trump. Would partner lead a singleton with only one trump in his hand? More likely, partner has ♣Q J and maybe another small club or two.

What card do you play to trick one?

Partner has not got ♣K when he leads the ♣Q, but declarer could have singleton ♣K. Win your ♣A now. Declarer plays the ♣2. WE have no more clubs to take, as dummy can ruff the third round.

Where are three more tricks coming from?

With only one spade trick, we need two more. Partner probably has ♦A or ♥A but not both. If he has either, you can get a diamond ruff.

What do you play to trick two?

♦8. Partner wins ♦A and leads ♦7 (a suit preference signal). You ruff.

What do you lead now?

The ♠3. Your partner wins and gives you another diamond ruff.

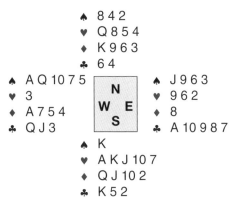

```
              ♠ 8 4 2
              ♥ Q 8 5 4
              ♦ K 9 6 3
              ♣ 6 4
♠ A Q 10 7 5      N        ♠ J 9 6 3
♥ 3           W       E    ♥ 9 6 2
♦ A 7 5 4         S        ♦ 8
♣ Q J 3                    ♣ A 10 9 8 7
              ♠ K
              ♥ A K J 10 7
              ♦ Q J 10 2
              ♣ K 5 2
```

What lessons do we learn from this deal?

Declarer has the 17 points you expected and partner has 13.

Partner's spade holding is as unattractive as you surmised. Leading ♠A could easily give a trick to declarer's king. Here it would drop the singleton king so it does not give a trick. But equally, it won't beat 4♥.

A singleton trump is rarely a good lead: it so often ruins partner's holding. An ace high diamond suit is not normally a good lead although here it could work out all right, if West leads another diamond. So ♣Q looks to be the best lead. It might set up club winners.

Since a singleton ♣K is always a possibility, you must win ♣A. Even if partner can ruff a club, two more tricks are needed to beat 4♥.

How does partner know that your switch to ♦8 is a singleton? Looking at dummy, partner would expect you to switch to a spade. Why should you want to play a diamond? Once partner realises you have done something unexpected, it is not so hard to work out why.

When partner gives you a diamond ruff, he should do so by leading ♦7. This high diamond is a suit preference signal, indicating that you should return a spade, rather than a club.

Case study 8

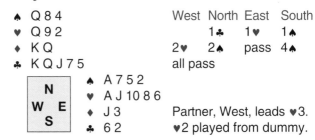

	♠ Q 8 4	West	North	East	South
	♥ Q 9 2		1♣	1♥	1♠
	♦ K Q	2♥	2♠	pass	4♠
	♣ K Q J 7 5	all pass			

	♠ A 7 5 2
	♥ A J 10 8 6
	♦ J 3
	♣ 6 2

Partner, West, leads ♥3.
♥2 played from dummy.

What are your first thoughts? What do you make of the lead?

Partner has supported hearts and led ♥3. He need only have three hearts as your overcall showed five, but his hearts will include an honour. You can see ♥A Q J 10 so partner must have ♥K.

You have ten and dummy has 15 points. Declarer jumped straight to game, so will have at least eleven, say the minor suit aces and ♠K.

If declarer has all the missing high cards, has the defence any chance?

Your one chance is that declarer has only five trumps and that you can make him ruff enough times in hearts, so that he runs out of trumps.

So what do you play to tricks one and two?

Play the ♥10 to trick one and the ♥A to trick two. The second heart wins as partner only had three hearts, ♥K 4 3.

What do you play to trick three?

A third heart which declarer ruffs to play a trump to dummy's ♠Q.

What do you do?

To make declarer run out of trumps, you must make him ruff another heart. If you win the first spade, dummy can take the heart ruff, which keeps declarer's trump length intact. Duck ♠Q and the next trump too. Declarer plays a third trump, which you win.

What do you play now?

Play a heart and force out declarer's last trump. Your ♠7 is now the only trump left. Use it as soon as you can and cash a heart winner.

This was the complete deal:

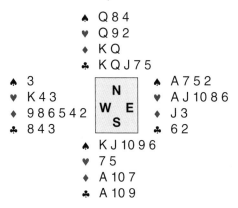

```
              ♠ Q 8 4
              ♥ Q 9 2
              ♦ K Q
              ♣ K Q J 7 5
♠ 3                              ♠ A 7 5 2
♥ K 4 3          N               ♥ A J 10 8 6
♦ 9 8 6 5 4 2  W   E             ♦ J 3
♣ 8 4 3          S               ♣ 6 2
              ♠ K J 10 9 6
              ♥ 7 5
              ♦ A 10 7
              ♣ A 10 9
```

What lessons do we learn from this deal?

You were right to overcall 1♥ on just ten points. Partner did well to raise with a bit of shape, taking up bidding space and making North rebid 2♠ rather than 1NT.

The overcall ensured that the best lead was found. East could see that a forcing defence would work if declarer had only five trumps. The contract must be unbeatable if declarer has six spades.

It is not enough for East to play another heart when he takes ♠A. He also has to make sure that dummy is out of spades, so that it is only declarer who can ruff the fourth heart. Winning the first or second round of spades won't work because dummy will have a trump left. It has to be the third round. See pages 91–92.

Declarer might abandon trumps when you have ducked ♠A twice and play on clubs instead. But if West plays his clubs upwards, that is giving a count signal to show an odd number of cards, you will know that South has a third club left and that you can safely ruff the third club for the setting trick.

Many players think there is no point in leading a suit that declarer can ruff. This hand shows exactly why it is very often right to keep leading a suit that the long trump hand, but not the short trump hand, can ruff.

Case study 9

```
♠ 9 4                              North  South
♥ Q J 9 4                                  1NT
♦ K 6 2                            2♣     2♥
♣ A Q J 7                          4♥
```

```
        N          ♠ A 7 5 2
   W    E          ♥ A 8 6
        S          ♦ J 7 5 4 3    Partner, West, leads ♠K.
                   ♣ 6            Dummy plays ♠4.
```

What are your first thoughts? What do you make of the lead?

Partner's lead is the top of a sequence of spade honours. He will have at least ♠K Q and quite possibly ♠K Q J. There are two spade tricks to take, but no more, as dummy can ruff the third round.

Dummy has 13 points, you have nine and declarer will have 12–14 points, leaving about five points for partner. You have already seen ♠K and assume he has ♠Q, so you cannot expect partner to have ♥K or ♦A.

Where might the four defensive tricks come from?

If the contract cannot be beaten by high card strength, it will have to be beaten by ruffs. If clubs are played at trick two, before trumps are drawn, you could ruff the second round.

How will partner know to play a club at trick two?

Partner cannot possibly know that you have a singleton club but you do.

How can you tell partner what to do?

There is no signal you could make which says 'Play a club'. You must overtake the ♠K with your ♠A and switch to a club! Declarer wins the club in dummy and leads ♥4.

What do you play on the ♥4?

Rise with ♥A and play a spade to partner's ♠Q. It should be very clear to partner to play a club for you to ruff.

Here is the complete deal:

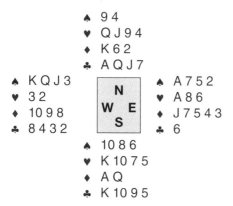

```
              ♠ 9 4
              ♥ Q J 9 4
              ♦ K 6 2
              ♣ A Q J 7
  ♠ K Q J 3              ♠ A 7 5 2
  ♥ 3 2         N        ♥ A 8 6
  ♦ 10 9 8   W     E     ♦ J 7 5 4 3
  ♣ 8 4 3 2     S        ♣ 6
              ♠ 10 8 6
              ♥ K 10 7 5
              ♦ A Q
              ♣ K 10 9 5
```

What lessons do we learn from this deal?

The bidding was correct; 3NT is bound to fail, losing four spades and one heart. The fact that 4♥ also went down was due to sharp defence and an unlucky distribution.

West had an easy opening lead. The 3-card sequence of ♠K Q J is always a good lead. It sets up winners and gives information to partner about where West's points are located.

From the lead East could build a picture of the whole hand. If his partner had five or six points in spades, as shown by the lead, it was extremely unlikely he had any more. Don't hope West has ♥K or ♦A.

East is the only player who knows that he has a singleton club. East knows that a club ruff is possible. How can West possibly tell? So East must find a way to help his partner to the correct defence. Once that is realised, overtaking the ♠K and playing the club must be the solution.

The ♠K lead made it easy for East to find partner's entry: it had to be ♠Q. West now has all the clues to win ♠Q and play a club.

At the table East played ♠2 at trick one and then queried why his partner had not found the club switch. But ♠2 is not a suit preference signal for clubs, it expresses East's attitude to the spade lead. When one defender knows what must be done, he must find a way to take control of the defence.

Case study 10

♠ A 4
♥ 8 7 2
♦ A K 7 4 3
♣ K J 10

	North	South
		1♠
	2♦	2♠
	3♣	3♠
	4♠	

```
      N        ♠ J 2
  W       E    ♥ A 3
      S        ♦ 10 9 8 2     Partner, West, leads ♥K.
               ♣ 9 8 4 3 2    Dummy plays ♥2.
```

What are your first thoughts? What do you make of the lead?

With 15 points, dummy is good for his bidding. South will normally have at least twelve points and will probably have six spades.

As you have five points, partner has at most eight. On ♥K lead, you know six of those points are ♥K Q J. Partner cannot have ♣A as well.

What do you play to trick one?

To make sure of cashing all the heart tricks your side is entitled to, you must play ♥A on partner's ♥K. It may hurt you to waste your honour, but if you play low, partner will play another heart and you will be stuck on lead with nothing sensible to play.

What do you play back after winning ♥A?

Having won ♥A you play ♥3, of course. Partner wins with ♥9. Both dummy and declarer started with three hearts, so that is three defensive tricks. Can you see any hope of a fourth?

What do you play on the third heart?

Prospects are not that good. The only realistic hope is the trump suit and your holding won't win any tricks. Probably best is to throw ♣2 to let partner know you have nothing useful in clubs.

Partner plays a fourth heart, ♥9. What is he doing?

Partner is playing for a trump promotion, our best chance. Whether or not dummy ruffs the heart, you must ruff as high as you can. Play ♠J.

Here is the complete deal.

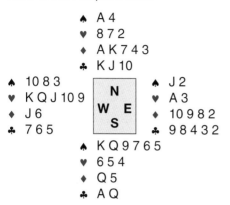

```
              ♠ A 4
              ♥ 8 7 2
              ♦ A K 7 4 3
              ♣ K J 10
♠ 10 8 3          N          ♠ J 2
♥ K Q J 10 9                 ♥ A 3
♦ J 6        W       E       ♦ 10 9 8 2
♣ 7 6 5          S           ♣ 9 8 4 3 2
              ♠ K Q 9 7 6 5
              ♥ 6 5 4
              ♦ Q 5
              ♣ A Q
```

What lessons do we learn from this deal?

The bidding was absolutely normal and opponents are unlucky to both have three hearts each, with ♥K being the obvious lead.

Look how important it is to read the information conveyed by the lead. ♥K shows ♥Q as well so East can confidently overtake with ♥A and play a heart back. Even if South had started with ♥J 10 9, East would be able to ruff the third round of hearts, so nothing is lost by playing ♥A at trick one.

Once East throws ♣2 on the third heart, West knows that there are no tricks available in the minors. A trump promotion is the only chance. Any spade honour in the East hand will do. In fact, ♠J 2 facing West's ♠10 8 3 is the minimum holding to promote a trick. There is nothing declarer can do about it.

Case study 11

```
    ♠ 9 6 4
    ♥ Q 5 3
    ♦ Q 6
    ♣ A K J 5 3
♠ Q 10 2
♥ 9 8            N
♦ J 7 5 4 3    W   E
♣ 6 4 2          S
```

West	North	East	South
		1♥	1♠
pass	3♠	pass	4♠
all pass			

As West, what do you lead?

Partner opened the bidding with 1♥. For once, you have an easy lead of ♥9, top card of a doubleton.

What are your first thoughts? Are you happy with the lead?

Dummy has twelve points, enough to bid 3♠. The spade holding is thin, just ♠9 6 4. Even though South promised five spades for the overcall, one would rather have slightly better support.

The lead looks good through dummy's ♥Q. Indeed it is, for partner wins ♥J at trick one, cashes ♥K and continues with ♥A. South ruffs the heart with ♠J.

What do you do?

If partner had already taken three tricks, you would overruff and get declarer one down. But here the overruff would only be the third defensive trick. It is hard to see where the fourth trick is coming from.

Given the good advice on page 97, of not overruffing with a certain trump trick, you should discard ♦3.

Declarer plays three rounds of spades and you are on lead after winning ♠Q. Partner only had one spade and discards ♥2 and ♦2. It wasn't a trump promotion hand, as you might have hoped.

What do you lead now?

Either a diamond or a club could be right but partner's discards give you a clue. Partner is strongly suggesting that you lead a club. Play ♣4.

Here is the complete deal:

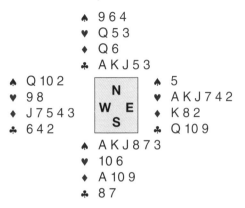

```
              ♠  9 6 4
              ♥  Q 5 3
              ♦  Q 6
              ♣  A K J 5 3
♠ Q 10 2                      ♠  5
♥ 9 8           N            ♥  A K J 7 4 2
♦ J 7 5 4 3   W   E          ♦  K 8 2
♣ 6 4 2         S            ♣  Q 10 9
              ♠  A K J 8 7 3
              ♥  10 6
              ♦  A 10 9
              ♣  8 7
```

What lessons do we learn from this deal?

Firstly, it is easier to find a good lead when partner has bid. West might have tried a fatal fourth highest diamond as his opening lead otherwise.

Secondly, East must continue leading hearts to tricks two and three. This ensures a trump trick is promoted if West has ♠Jxx or ♠10xxx.

Thirdly, it is nearly always wrong to overruff with a sure trump trick even if the reason is hard to see. Suppose you do overruff and exit with a club. Declarer wins ♣A and cashes ♠A K, drawing your two remaining trumps. Then a club to ♣K and a club ruff establishes two winners in dummy, with ♠9 as entry to cash them.

Fourthly, even if West does not overruff, declarer still has chances. West might have led back a diamond after winning the trump trick. Playing low from dummy would catch East's ♦K. East knows that a club lead will beat the contract whether or not declarer takes the club finesse, since there is no entry to dummy's club winners even if they are set up. So East must do his best to signal to ensure that a club is led.

Case study 12

```
♠ 8 4
♥ A 5 2
♦ 4 3
♣ K J 10 8 7 3
```

	North	South
		1♦
	2♣	3NT

```
        ♠ 9 7 6 2
   N    ♥ K 3
 W   E  ♦ J 10 8 5      Partner, West, leads ♥6.
   S    ♣ A Q 2         Dummy plays ♥2.
```

What are your first thoughts?

With just eight points, dummy has nothing to spare for his bidding. Declarer has shown 17–19 points by jumping to 3NT. You have ten so partner could have five points at most.

Partner looks to have found a good lead; it could knock out dummy's entry to the long clubs. You win ♥K and return ♥3 but declarer wins ♥Q and plays ♣4. Partner plays ♣9 and dummy plays ♣10.

How do you plan to defend ?

Partner's ♣9 may be a singleton, in which case declarer has three clubs. Or it may be the start of a high-low count signal to show a doubleton (see page 45–49), in which case declarer has only two clubs.

Either way, it cannot cost to duck and let dummy's ♣10 win the trick. Declarer returns to hand with a diamond and plays another club. Partner produces ♣6, so he did have a doubleton and so did declarer. You win ♣Q, feeling pleased with your defence so far.

What do you do now?

You have a choice of playing spades or diamonds. Whilst your diamonds are stronger, they are the suit declarer bid first. Switch to spades, leading through strength and up to dummy's weakness.

Play ♠7, second highest from a poor suit.

Here is the complete deal:

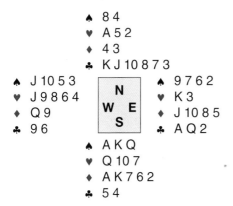

```
                  ♠ 8 4
                  ♥ A 5 2
                  ♦ 4 3
                  ♣ K J 10 8 7 3
  ♠ J 10 5 3                      ♠ 9 7 6 2
  ♥ J 9 8 6 4      N              ♥ K 3
  ♦ Q 9         W     E           ♦ J 10 8 5
  ♣ 9 6            S              ♣ A Q 2
                  ♠ A K Q
                  ♥ Q 10 7
                  ♦ A K 7 6 2
                  ♣ 5 4
```

What lessons do we learn from this deal?

The bidding was normal. Although North has only eight points, the 6-card club suit adds value to the hand. South has 18 points and a 5-card diamond suit, well worth a jump to 3NT. On a good day West would hold ♣Q and the contract is unbeatable.

West had a natural heart lead, even though the suit is fairly poor and the hand is unlikely to have an entry. There is really no reason to lead anything else.

Of course, the crucial play on the hand is East's ducking of the club. This was made easier by West's count signal to show two clubs and suggesting the declarer might only have two clubs too. It very rarely costs a trick to duck the club in this position, see page 46. It is fairly clear that declarer will need to bring the clubs in to make the contract.

When the club is ducked, South is always going to repeat the finesse. When this fails, he would still have made the contract had the diamonds broken 3-3. But when they were 4-2, East makes two clubs, two diamonds and a heart for one down.

index of key words